CW00497713
Lothian
40 favourite Walks

The author and publisher have made every effort to ensure that the information in this publication is accurate, and accept no responsibility whatsoever for any loss, injury or inconvenience experienced by any person or persons whilst using this book.

published by
pocket mountains ltd
The Old Church, Annanside,
Moffat, Dumfries and Galloway DG10 9HB

ISBN: 978-1-907025-72-3

A catalogue record for this book is available from the British Library

Printed in Poland

ntroduction

:ting to the west of Edinburgh, ndwiched between the southern shore the Firth of Forth and the ever-present ajesty of the western Pentlands, West thian is often passed through on the 3 from Edinburgh to Glasgow or on the) to Stirling and the West Highlands.

Those who speed through this untingly beautiful county, however, e missing some of the finest scenery in wland Scotland. The lochs and forests the Bathgate Hills are a veritable ossachs in miniature; the view from the p of Cockleroy Hill, right across otland's Central Belt from the Isle of ay in the east to the Isle of Arran in the st, and northwest to Ben Ledi and the al Trossachs, is a true panorama.

story

ehistoric Stone Age and Bronze Age habitants, the Romans, kings and eens of both Scotland and England, venanters, Jacobites and industrialists ve all left their mark on the county. The ouse of Stewart, probably the greatest yal dynasty in British history, built its lace at Linlithgow and its most famous ember, the ill-fated Mary, Queen of ots, was born there.

This guide touches upon two UNESCO orld Heritage Sites, at the Antonine Wall Bo'ness and the Forth Bridge at South eensferry. Neither of these are now part West Lothian but as the county was ginally designated, taking the Rivers Avon and Almond as its natural boundaries, this is their home.

It could also be argued that the Industrial Revolution began here, in a small unassuming workshop on Kinneil Estate where in 1769 inventor James Watt first started work on a steam engine that would revolutionise the industrial world.

Centuries earlier, the monks of Holyrood Abbey had discovered coal in the hillside above Bo'ness, beginning 800 years of mining in the county. But West Lothian remained largely agricultural, with weaving and distilling being the main industries until James 'Paraffin' Young invented a process to extract crude oil from shale in the mid-19th century and triggered the world's first oil boom.

The subsequent industries that grew up in the 18th, 19th and 20th centuries have left their mark on the landscape. The huge mounds of spent shale, or 'bings' (from the Gaelic *beinn* for 'hill' or 'mountain') – the waste product of Young's process – are now listed structures which are being reinvented as wildlife havens, while many of the railway lines that served these long-gone industries are now walking trails.

The Union Canal which linked with the Forth & Clyde Canal at Falkirk in 1790 and boasts three great aqueducts – over the Water of Leith at Slateford, the River Almond near Ratho and the River Avon by Linlithgow – as well as 62 bridges, also eventually fell into decline with the opening of the Edinburgh to Glasgow

Railway in 1841, though in the last twenty years the canal has been revived for recreational use.

The last shale oil mine closed in 1962 but as one door closes, another opens. Like a phoenix from the ashes of West Lothian's industrial past, Livingston has grown from a small village to the largest town in the Lothians, second in size only to the city of Edinburgh itself, and it is now home to new industries of electronics and communications, as well as being a popular commuter town for Edinburgh.

Geography and geology

West Lothian is sometimes described as 'Corridor County', because the main routes through it have always run east to west, from Edinburgh to Glasgow, Stirling or the north. From the coastal plain of the Forth at Bo'ness, the ground rises before dropping down to the valley at Linlithgow. Almost immediately south of here, the Bathgate Hills form another natural barrier before sloping down to the broad Almond Valley at Bathgate and Livingston. Finally, the Pentland Hills, forced up when two ancient continents collided more than 400 million years ago, border West Lothian's southern limits from Edinburgh towards Lanarkshire.

Most of this area is underlaid by sedimentary rocks – Devonian sandstones from ancient deserts, Carboniferous sandstone from rivers and mudstones, coal from ancient peat bogs and forests and limestones from prehistoric seas and lakes. Around 350 million years ago, muc of West Lothian was a vast tropical lagoon. The mud that settled on the bottom of the lagoon was rich in dead plants and animals that decomposed ov time to form kerogen-bearing oil shale.

Today's landscape is also a result of ancient volcanic eruptions laying down lava flows and ash which was then worn down during the ice ages when even the ice flowed through West Lothian from west to east, leaving the distinctive volcanic crag and tail formations at Binn Craig and Dechmont Law. The River Fort itself is a fjord carved by the ice, its islands simply more crag and tails. Ice eroded the Pentlands too, reducing then in height from more than 1500m to less than 600m. When the ice finally receded, peat bogs formed across West Lothian, particularly around the southwest.

How to use this guide

This guide contains forty short to moderate walks, all of which can be completed in less than half a day. There excellent public transport within West Lothian and regular bus services to the start of many of the routes.

Three railway lines run through West Lothian. Hop on the Edinburgh to Glasgow Queen Street train for Linlithgow. The Bathgate Line also runs from Edinburgh to Glasgow Queen Stree and may be used for routes near Uphall Station, Livingston North, Bathgate, Armadale and Blackridge. Finally, take th

dinburgh to Glasgow Central Line for
outes near Kirknewton, Livingston South
nd Fauldhouse. A fourth line, from
dinburgh to Fife via the Forth Bridge,
ops at Dalmeny, the railway station
r South Queensferry.

Most of the routes are low level with
w, if any, steep climbs, and take
dvantage of the network of paths left
ehind by West Lothian's rich industrial
ast. Many, particularly those that
corporate the country parks at
mondell, Beecraigs and Polkemmet,
e suitable for children or for elderly
alkers. Most of the routes are on formal
aths, quiet country roads and woodland
acks, and any steep, awkward or boggy
rrain is noted.

For the longer walks, particularly on the
oors, you should always carry an OS
ap and compass and know how to use
em. Many walkers use Global
ositioning Systems (GPS) these days,
ut GPS signals can be lost and phones
n run out of power. GPS can tell you
here you are but cannot tell you where
go next in conditions of poor visibility.

In winter, be prepared for the
hallenges of poor weather and shortened
aylight hours. At any time of year,
alking conditions can change. Wet
eather can quickly turn an unsurfaced
otpath into a quagmire and steeper
opes can become slippery with mud.
rong winds too, particularly on higher
ound and on coastal walks at high tide,
n be dangerous.

Preparation for your walk begins at home. Choose a route that reflects your abilities and dress appropriately for the weather and the terrain: this is Scotland and carrying warm, waterproof clothing is generally advisable, even if you don't need it. Walking shoes are fine for the lower-level walks but good quality walking boots are recommended for the hills, and walking poles are always handy, regardless of the terrain.

Access

The Land Reform (Scotland) Act of 2003 gives members of the public a right to access most Scottish land and inland waters, and landowners have a responsibility not to unreasonably prevent or deter access. However, key to the Act is that members of the public exercise their rights responsibly, as laid out in the Scottish Outdoor Access Code (www.outdooraccess-scotland.com).

This includes taking your litter home with you and respecting the environment and private property. Do not damage fences and crops, and close all gates behind you.

Dogs should be kept under strict control, particularly in the spring and early summer when they could disturb groundnesting birds. Do not enter a field with your dog if there are lambs, calves or other young farm animals and at any time keep your dog on a short lead in fields with livestock.

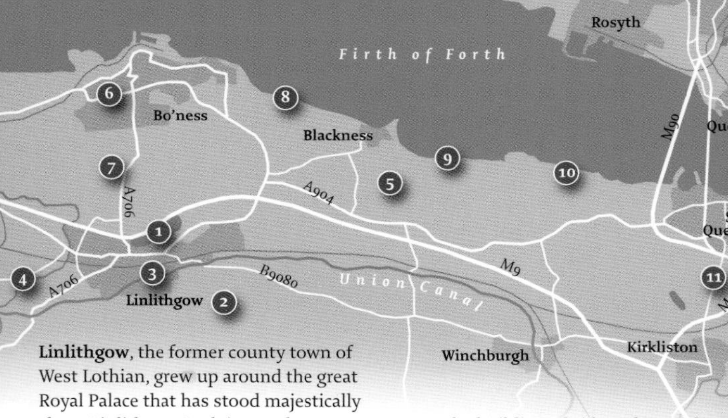

Linlithgow, the former county town of West Lothian, grew up around the great Royal Palace that has stood majestically above Linlithgow Loch in one form or another for nearly 900 years. Sandwiched between the Bathgate Hills in the south and the Erngath Hills in the north, with the valley of the River Avon to the west, it is almost impossible to walk around the town without encountering either the loch or the Union Canal, which slices across the south of Linlithgow on its way to Falkirk.

Across the Erngath Hills from Linlithgow, the Firth of Forth bites inland, almost cutting Scotland in two. The estuary was excavated by glaciers, scouring deep basins in the landscape during the last ice age and carving out the steep hills that rise above the historic ports of Bo'ness, Blackness and Queensferry.

These days, the Firth is spanned at Queensferry, but in times past, the Forth estuary has proven to be an effective barrier against invaders from the south, forcing them upstream to Stirling where a castle defended the route north. The Romans, under the command of Septimius Severus, solved the problem in 207AD by building a bridge of around 900 boats across the Forth, probably at Queensferry, as they attempted to subdu Scotland. The Antonine Wall, stretching westwards across Scotland from Bo'ness became their base, and only the death of Severus in York in 211AD prevented the Romans from capitalising on the blitzkrieg that was unleashed on the Caledonian tribes.

The estuary is important for nature conservation and the stretch between Bo'ness and Abercorn is a designated Sit of Special Scientific Interest with more than 90,000 breeding seabirds every year it has international significance as a site for birds from as far afield as Scandinavi Iceland and the Arctic, who spend their winters on and around the mudflats at Bo'ness. Look out for wading birds such as redshanks, knots, dunlins and oystercatchers. Peregrine falcons hunt along the shoreline, and if you are lucky you may witness hundreds of birds take to the skies as they are flushed out from the ground cover and hedgerows.

Linlithgow and the Forth shore

Linlithgow Loch circular

Distance 3.7km Time 1 hour
Terrain mostly surfaced footpaths, with one short unsurfaced track
Map OS Explorer 349 Access regular bus and rail services to Linlithgow

This is one of West Lothian's most popular walks, although no less enjoyable for that, as the route around Linlithgow Loch is packed with wildlife and historical interest.

The loch and its palace are undoubtedly the jewel in the historic burgh's crown, so it is fitting that Linlithgow's name derives from the Brythonic for 'Loch in the Damp Hollow'. The largest of two remaining natural Lowland lochs in the Lothians, it was formed when a kettle hole filled with glacial meltwater at the end of the last ice age. Despite its considerable surface area, Linlithgow Loch is unexpectedly shallow, with its depth ranging from an average of just over 2m to a maximum of 9m.

This walk starts at St Ninian's Way Car Park, accessed by road off St Ninian's Road at the west end of the loch or on foot from the High Street. A short path leads to the water's edge where you turn left to follow the path clockwise around the loch. After passing through a willow tree archway, you'll see the grazing land of Lady's Park and Calf Lea, which is protected from development, on the left.

Bear right after the little bridge over the Mill Lade to soon reach the northern shore, a designated Site of Special Scientific Interest (SSSI). The trees that grow here are home to many species of birds, mammals and insects. Small birds shelter in the gorse and broom around the base of the trees while the meadow is home to butterflies, bees and small mammals such as rabbits, mice and voles.

The islands on the loch are the remains of two 2000-year-old man-made crannogs which supported wooden houses. These

Linlithgow Palace from the Peel

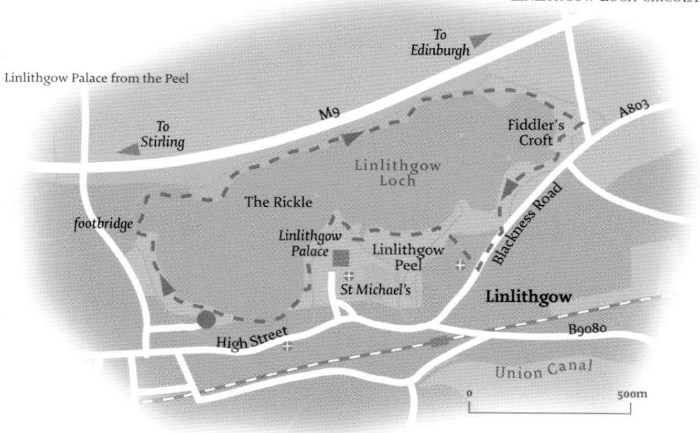

ere probably built by important families r display and status, with the additional enefit that they were difficult to attack.

Continue along the northern shore to ach a road, turning immediately right to ıter an area known as Fiddler's Croft via gate. The boggy shore is a mass of water rget-me-not, marsh marigold and eadowsweet in season, attracting a riety of bees and butterflies, while ebes, coots, swans and ducks nest nongst the reeds.

To complete the circuit of the loch, you ıve to leave the shore temporarily: at a ite exit onto Blackness Road and head ght, back towards the town centre, rning right again down a lane at the ext signpost to return to Linlithgow Peel ıe park); swing left towards the palace.

Linlithgow has been a Royal Burgh ıce David I built a hunting lodge on the e of Linlithgow Palace in the 1100s. tuated halfway between the castles at linburgh and Stirling, it made an ideal overnight stay, saving the monarch the bother of returning to either of these castles after a long day's hunting.

The present palace was begun by James I in 1424, with subsequent additions by James III, James IV and James V. Mary, Queen of Scots was born here in 1524. Royalty left the palace in 1603 when James VI moved his court to London following the Union of the Crowns. The last of the Stewarts to stay at the palace was Charles I, who spent the night in 1633. When Bonnie Prince Charlie stayed in 1745, the fountain in the courtyard flowed with wine in his honour. But it was set alight by the troops of the Duke of Cumberland following their defeat by the Jacobites at the Battle of Falkirk in January 1746.

At a crosspaths, turn right to head around the peninsula, down the hill and through a gateway. Continue along the southern shore of the loch, passing beneath several huge willow trees to arrive back at the car park.

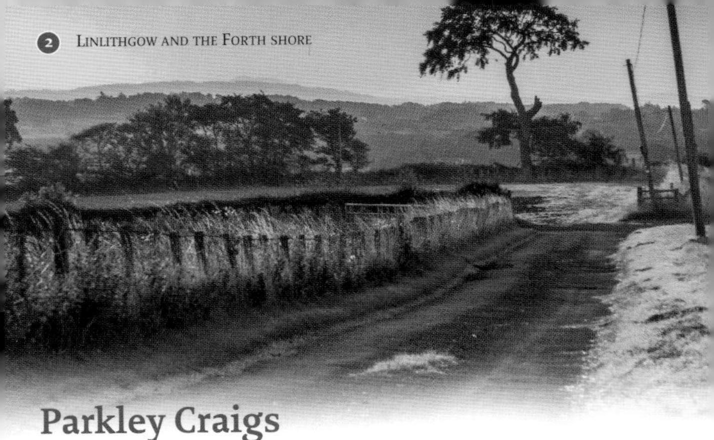

Parkley Craigs

Distance **6.4km** Time **1 hour 45**
Terrain **mostly surfaced tracks and roads, one short unsurfaced track, one steep hill**
Map **OS Explorer 349** Access **regular bus and rail services to Linlithgow**

Head out of Linlithgow along the former towpath of the Union Canal and into the lower slopes of the Bathgate Hills.

The walk starts in the Regent Centre Car Park in Linlithgow. The car park is built on the site of the former Regent Works, which were named after James Stuart, Regent of Scotland, who was assassinated on Linlithgow High Street in 1570. They were opened in 1902 by Nobel's Explosives a year after the first Nobel Peace Prize was awarded as instructed in the will of company founder, the Swedish chemist and engineer, Alfred Noble.

When the factory was demolished in 1982, a time capsule containing newspapers, documents and coins, which had been buried during the original opening ceremony, was discovered. It wa buried again in a new capsule detailing life in Linlithgow during the 1980s.

Facing back towards Blackness Road from the entrance to the car park, shortc across the shopping precinct to the left. Exit onto Blackness Road, turn left and cross at the roundabout to the Star and Garter pub. Just past here, turn left uphil to the railway station.

Built in 1842, this is one of the best-preserved stations on the Edinburgh to Glasgow Mainline, the first passenger railway in Scotland which opened just 13 years after George Stephenson's Rock won the Rainhill Trials in Lancashire, ushering in the age of steam travel. The station is the subject of what is thought to be the world's earliest photograph of railway station, in a daguerreotype taken from the towpath of the Union Canal by Scottish artist David Octavius Hill and chemist Robert Adamson in 1845.

Walk beneath the railway and up the hi

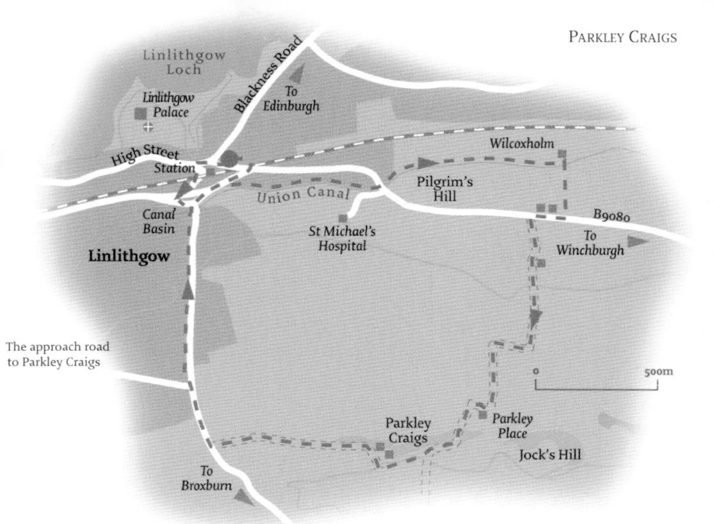

The approach road to Parkley Craigs

urning right at the top and crossing the ɔad to the canal basin. A bronze sculpture f a cat named *Dudley* sits on a plinth by ne canal as a memorial to a founding ıember of Linlithgow's Burgh Beautiful ʼho owned a cat by this name.

Turn left to head eastwards out of town, rossing the canal at Bridge 42 and ɔllowing the farm track to the main road. ere, double back towards town for 100m r so, then take the minor road that strikes ff uphill to the left, signposted for Parkley arm. There are superb views from the top f the hill with Grangemouth visible in the istance to the west, Stuc a'Chroin on the orizon and the Ochils, the Forth, the ɔwer at the House of the Binns and the orth Bridges over in the east. The athgate Hills are to the south with ockleroy prominent in the southwest nd Binny Craig in the southeast.

Walk through a farm before veering right to pass in front of and around a cottage and past some holiday cottages. Immediately after a sharp left turn, a track leads off through the trees on the right to pass some stables before joining another farm track. The track swings right up the hill, becoming a road almost immediately. This is the hamlet of Parkley Craigs, comprised of a few farm buildings that have been converted into homes.

Follow the road up the hill to meet with the main Manse Road. Turn right to head down into Linlithgow again. At the bridge over the canal, turn right to drop down the hill past the station car park and under the railway line beyond. Cross the road immediately under the bridge, go through a gap in the wall and down a set of concrete steps to return to the car park.

The Perambulation of the Marches

Distance 6.9km **Time** 1 hour 45
Terrain mostly formal footpaths, occasional unsurfaced tracks
Map OS Explorer 349 **Access** regular bus and rail services to Linlithgow

This town walk follows the route of the Parliamentary Boundary of the Royal Burgh of Linlithgow. The Boundary is marked by eight March Stones (one original and seven replicas), inscribed 'LPB' (Linlithgow Parliamentary Burgh). Spotting the stones can be great entertainment for younger children.

The first stone is in front of St Ninian's Craigmailen Church just beyond the West Port in Linlithgow. From here return towards the town centre, turning left to head up Philip Avenue and down the lane at the end of the road. Cross St Ninian's Road and turn left to pass the second stone beside the path. Just after the stone, walk down to Linlithgow Loch and over the Mill Lade bridge. This outlet once supplie Lochmill, one of two local paper mills.

Go around the loch towards the palace, passing residents and visitors who gathe to feed the birdlife. Head through a gate in the wall and around the north of the palace. This grassy area is Linlithgow Pee one of two Royal Parks in Scotland; the other is Holyrood Park in Edinburgh. Bea left across the peel and then divert up a lane to the main Blackness Road. Turn le along this road and left again at a gate to return to the loch at Fiddler's Croft. Look out for the third stone tucked behind a bench on the left.

After another gate, turn right onto a minor road to return to Blackness Road and head briefly back towards town before turning up Springfield Road. Ston number four is in the grass on the right. Turn down the street numbered 16-24 an along the path at the end, turning right and then left to skirt around the cricket

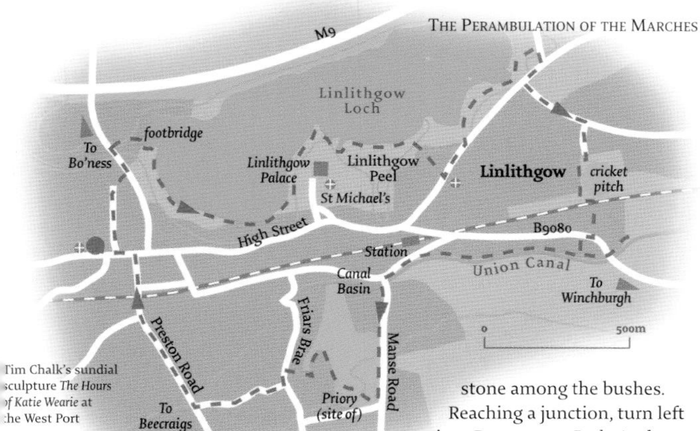

Tim Chalk's sundial sculpture *The Hours of Katie Wearie* at the West Port

tch where West Lothian County Cricket ub have played since 1930.

From the club car park, follow the ad beneath the railway and up the hill Edinburgh Road. Head back briefly wards town before crossing over to llow a road uphill between two walls d climbing the steps to the Union nal. An optional short detour to the left kes you to the fifth stone, but the main ute goes west along the canal.

The buildings at Linlithgow Canal Basin e former stable blocks where the horses at pulled the canal boats were rested. oss Bridge 43 and walk up Manse Road, rning right into trees at a pair of teposts to find the scant remains of rmelite Friary, built in the early 15th ntury on land given to the order by Sir mes Douglas of Dalkeith; it was stroyed by the Reformers in 1559.

Continuing through the woods, look for e sixth (and only original surviving) stone among the bushes.

Reaching a junction, turn left into Rosemount Park. At the end of the path, turn left to walk across the grass through an attractive avenue of trees towards the end of Friar's Loan, just beside stone number seven.

Turn down this road and cross the main road. Turn left, then right along Priory Road, crossing Burgess Hill. At the next street follow the path between two houses to arrive at a bridge where Preston Road crosses the canal. The eighth stone is a little harder to spot than the others, tucked beneath the bridge.

Cross the road and head downhill, turning left onto the West Port at the bottom of the hill. On the left is Tim Chalk's 2011 sculpture of Katie Wearie. According to legend, Katie was a drover who washed her feet in the cattle trough on market days and then rested below a tree outside the West Port gate. The branches above Katie's head contain a bird, whose shadow traces the hours on the markings set into the ground, forming a sundial.

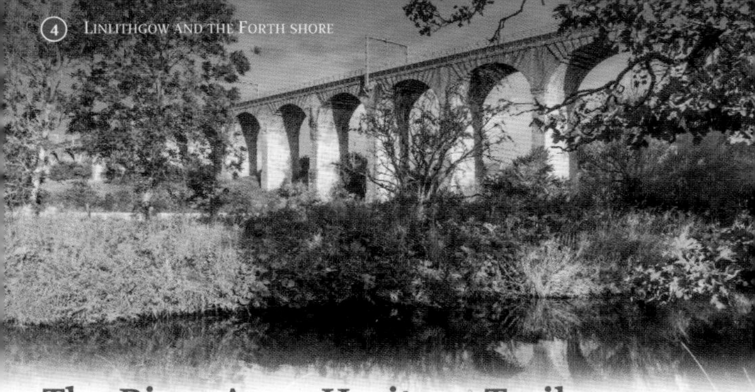

The River Avon Heritage Trail

Distance 13.4km Time 3 hours 30 (one way) Terrain unsurfaced tracks, some very muddy Map OS Explorer 349 Access this is a linear route which requires transport at each end, though it is possible to return by bus from the end, changing at Falkirk (check times before setting out)

This walk follows the River Avon along the western border of West Lothian from Avonbridge to Linlithgow, passing under two viaducts and Scotland's highest and longest aqueduct on the way. The Avon is a wildlife corridor, home to brown trout and salmon, otters and kingfishers.

From the Main Street in Avonbridge, head down the crescent of Bridgend Road, leaving it at the corner for a lane that leads on between fields before turning right on a narrow track to meet the River Avon. Follow the track over the Lin Mill Burn and on through a series of gates to cross the river at Strath Mill. Turn right along the road, then go through a gate to rejoin the riverside for the next very muddy section.

Climb the steps beneath the Westfield Viaduct which was built in 1855 and was in operation for little over a century; it ha since fallen into disrepair.

Continue along a field at the top of the gorge, then drop back down through tree emerging from them to cross a field and go through a gate at the far side. Pass ove a bridge to enter woods, cutting directly across a clearing, up steps and over the h to descend into a smaller gorge. Cross th burn and go down to a pretty little waterfall. The sandstone here contains fossilised Carboniferous tree trunks.

Walk along some duckboards to cross the Wallace Bridge. The adjacent sandstone arch, eroded by the river over thousands of years, is known as Wallace Cave as it was allegedly used by William Wallace to hide from English troops afte the Battle of Falkirk in 1298.

Turn right to climb uphill into woods, bearing left at a bench to descend steps and cross a bridge. Bear left again to cros a little stone bridge and walk through an

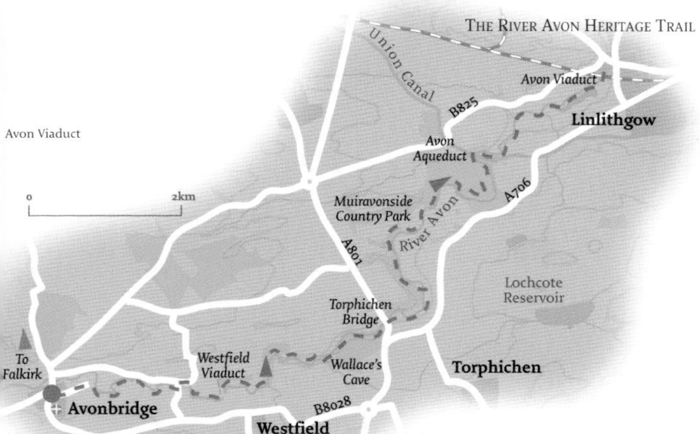

Avon Viaduct

ak and birch woodland incongruously alled the Desert – look out for willow varbler and whitethroat here.

Steps descend to a walkway beneath 'orphichen Bridge and through a gate nto a field. The solitary gable end at the ar end of the field marks the birthplace of teamship pioneer Henry Bell who aunched Britain's first steamboat, the *'omet*, in 1811.

Cross the Carribber Bridge to enter ʻluiravonside Country Park at Carribber ilen, designated a Site of Special cientific Interest because of its wealth f ground flora. Continue through a series f gates and bridges before climbing teeply out of the glen. At the top, bear ight to drop gently downhill and cross a ıeadow to join a woodland path.

Follow the sign for the car park to pass round the remains of Muiravonside Iouse. Built in 1604, the house was ought from the Stirling family by Falkirk ouncil in 1967 who demolished it and turned the estate into a country park. Turn right at the visitor centre and right again at the junction beyond the doocot, now home to a colony of bats. Look out for carved owls in the branches above.

Pass through the Stirling family burial ground, then drop down one set of steps before climbing another. Turn right near the top and go uphill at the old mill, bearing right to approach the towering Avon Aqueduct. Designed by Hugh Baird and Thomas Telford, the 250m-long, 26m-high aqueduct was completed in 1821 to carry the Union Canal across the Avon.

Keep right to climb the steps to the canal and cross the aqueduct. Turn left at a signpost to descend a series of walkways and bear left to continue along the side of the river. Soon, the Avon Viaduct comes into view. Completed in 1841, it is almost twice the length of the Avon Aqueduct. Cross another bridge to climb steps below the viaduct and go through a gate to Burgh Mills Lane and the end of the walk in Linlithgow.

The House of the Binns

Distance 3.2km Time 1 hour
Terrain mostly unsurfaced tracks, some roads, one very muddy section
Map OS Explorer 349 Access no public transport to the start

In 1601, Thomas Dalyell, a butter merchant from Edinburgh, was appointed Depute Master of the Rolls to James VI of Scotland and moved to London with the King following the Union of the Crowns in 1603. He returned north a rich man and purchased the Binns Estate and manor house. It has been home to the Baronetcy of Dalyell since 1685. The name of the estate is derived from the two *beinns*, or hills, upon which it is situated.

Thomas Dalyell's son, General Tam 'Bluidy' Dalyell, led the fight against the Covenanters in the 17th century. His enemies said that the General was in league with Satan himself and stories abounded of his dealings with the devil. Even his name was pronounced, 'De'il'. Following his death, his son became the first Baronet. The late politician Tam Dalyell was the 11th Baronet and lived at the Binns for his entire life. In 1944, the house, its contents and parkland were given to the National Trust for Scotland, although the right of the Dalyell family to live in the house was retained.

Beginning at the car park by the house, cross the road to the picnic area and take the path cut through the grass, continuing straight on at the junction to follow the sign for the woodland walk. In the spring, there are beautiful displays of snowdrops in this avenue. Take the steps up the hill and through a gate, climbing another set of steps to the tower.

Also known as Dalyell's Folly and The Wager, Binns Tower is the highest point for several miles. It was built as the result of a bet. Sir James Dalyell, the fifth Baronet, had a wager with his friends, the winner being the guest who could find

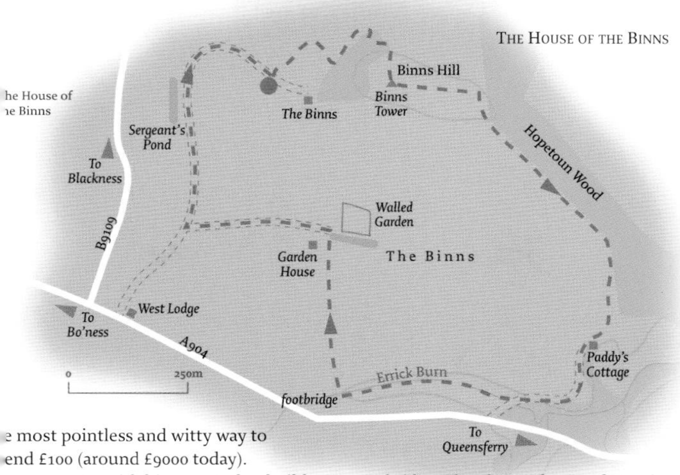

e most pointless and witty way to
end £100 (around £9000 today).
James won, with his proposal to build
ower on the top of Binns Hill
ecifically to be seen by and, more
portantly, to literally look down upon
s less aristocratic neighbours.
Strike out east along the ridge of the
l, turning right at the trees which mark
e boundary with the Hopetoun Estate,
follow the fence down the hill to a gate.
ntinue straight across the field towards
listant waymark post. Turn right at the
st to pass Paddy's Cottage. Once a
apel, as suggested by the cross, a
mhand named Paddy Gallagher made
is his home in the 1930s.
A road begins here, heading south to
n alongside the Errick Burn Wood
fore crossing the burn itself. This wet
odland is a haven for wildlife,
luding dippers. Leave the road through
gate on the right and follow a track
ng the south bank before crossing back
er on a wooden bridge beside a ruined
stone bridge. The ghost of General Tam is said to haunt The Binns. Mounted on a grey horse, as used by his Dragoons, he enters his estate before crossing this bridge and following the route of the original driveway up to the house, where he dismounts in the middle of the dining room, formerly the site of the courtyard.

Follow the track uphill through another three gates. The walled garden at the top of the hill, built around 1820, is where the Dalyells grew fruit, vegetables and flowers. Turn left to follow a road past the ruins of an old stable block and right at the junction, passing the Sergeant's Pond on the left. During the summer of 1870, a marble-topped table was recovered from the waters. It was said to have been thrown here by Satan himself after losing at cards to General Tam. The pond is also said to be haunted by a kelpie, known as Green Jeanie. Continue back up to the house and the start.

Kinneil and the Antonine Wall

Distance 8.6km Time 2 hours 15
Terrain surfaced paths, roadside paths and unsurfaced tracks
Map OS Explorer 349 Access regular bus services to Bo'ness from Linlithgow

Visit the northern frontier of the Roman Empire and the birthplace of the Industrial Revolution on a walk around the fringes of Bo'ness.

Begin from the winding wheel mining memorial near Bo'ness foreshore. There is a car park here, accessed just off Seaview Place at the west end of the town centre. Coalmining began in Bo'ness some 800 years ago and finally ended when Kinneil Colliery closed in 1984.

Cross the A904 and the railway, turning left to follow the path. The mudflats, squelched between the Bo'ness foreshore and the sea, have huge national and international importance and species such as mallard, teal, great crested grebe, curlew and knot can often be seen.

At an information board, follow the grassy track into Kinneil Nature Reserve jutting out into the sea on a man-made peninsula formed from material excavated from the colliery and planted with native species.

The track hugs the shoreline as it rounds the point to be unexpectedly greeted by a congestion of chimneys, pipes and cooling towers smoking acros the bay. This is Grangemouth – Scotland only oil refinery – established in 1924 by Scottish Oils, a merger of several of West Lothian's shale oil producers, to process crude oil shipped in from the Persian Gu

Leaving the headland, find the railway crossing and turn right on the other sid following John Muir Way signs to go across the grass, through a parking area and up Snab Lane. This lane continues the other side of the main road, heading up to the A993 where you carry on uphi before crossing and turning right onto t avenue of Kinneil House.

Now in the care of Historic Scotland, Kinneil House was once the principal se

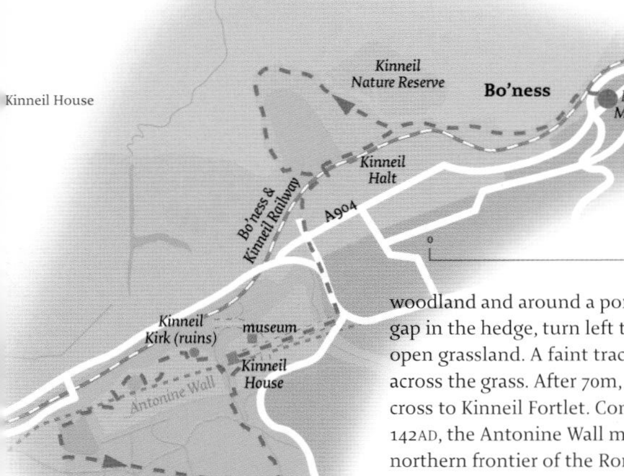

f the Hamilton family in the east of cotland and contains the most extensive nd best preserved 16th-century ceiling nd wall paintings in Scotland.

Go through a gap in the wall to the left f the house to reach the little ruined ottage where James Watt carried out his xperiments into using pressurised steam pump water from deep mines. His work ere led to the development of the ngines that would power industry for e next 150 years.

Cross the burn and walk along the vine at the back of Kinneil House to ach a ruined kirk. Dating from the 12th ntury, the kirk was in use until 1745 hen it was accidentally burnt down by agoons stationed there to protect nneil from the Jacobites.

Continue straight ahead along the track t through the grass, on through some woodland and around a pond. Beyond a gap in the hedge, turn left to emerge onto open grassland. A faint track heads west across the grass. After 70m, turn left to cross to Kinneil Fortlet. Constructed in 142AD, the Antonine Wall marked the northern frontier of the Roman Empire. Kinneil, which is Gaelic for 'Wall's End', was at its eastern end. The wall was added to the UNESCO World Heritage List in 2008.

Return to the path and continue west, climbing a set of steps. Bear left to take the path around the curling pond, eventually leaving it to follow a long straight path leading gently eastwards uphill, bearing right at a fork. At a crossroads just before the path enters mature woodland, head downhill through the trees.

This woodland was originally planted as a commercial enterprise between 1929 and 1949, but regular tree felling ceased when timber prices tumbled. Turn right at the bottom to walk through a small car park before following the John Muir Way back downhill to Watt's Cottage.

From here, retrace your steps down to the railway crossing and turn right. Turn right again to walk along the platform at Kinneil Halt, rejoining the path at the end to continue back to the start.

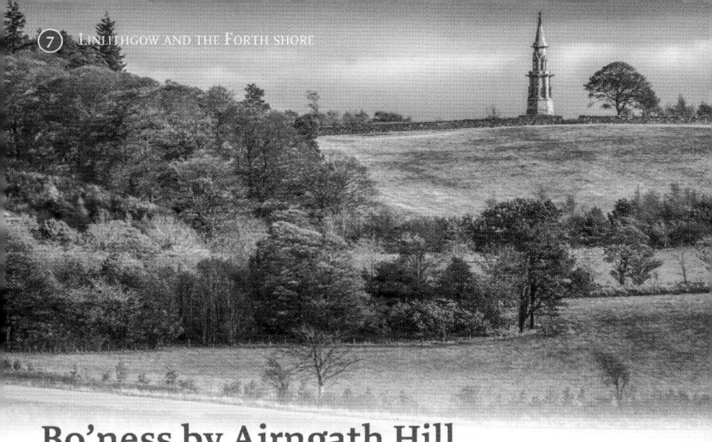

Bo'ness by Airngath Hill

Distance **15.8km** **Time** **4 hours**
Terrain **surfaced and unsurfaced paths, minor country roads, some steep climbs**
Map **OS Explorer 349** **Access** **regular bus and rail services to Linlithgow**

A traditional over-the-hill route between the historic towns of Linlithgow and Bo'ness with sweeping views across both, returning along the John Muir Way.

The route begins at the Cross Well off Linlithgow High Street. Constructed in 1806 by one-armed stonemason Robert Gray who worked with a mallet strapped to his stump, it was an exact replica of a well that had stood on the site since 1628, some 25 years after the Union of the Crowns, which is celebrated in the carvings.

Head up the Kirkgate, turning left beyond the palace gate towards the statue of Mary, Queen of Scots who was born here in 1542. Follow the path behind the palace, descending from the hill to continue by the loch and then up a lane t Blackness Road. Turn left here and left again at a gate to head through Fiddler's Croft to a second gate onto a minor road.

Turn left to follow the road uphill over the M9, going left again on a private road which climbs past the Grange, built by geographer and geologist Henry Moubray Cadell between 1904 and 1909. The estate had initially been leased by William Cade one of Scotland's early industrialists and founder of Falkirk's Carron Iron Works; th family bought the estate in 1778, exploitin it for its reserves of iron ore.

Keep left to follow the road as it loops up over Airngath Hill with stunning view back over Linlithgow. Turn right onto the public road at the far end to walk east for 700m with superb views to the Ochil Hill before taking the Public Right of Way downhill by the golf course and through a gate into a field. Carry on downhill, between stone gateposts and through a

The Hope Monument

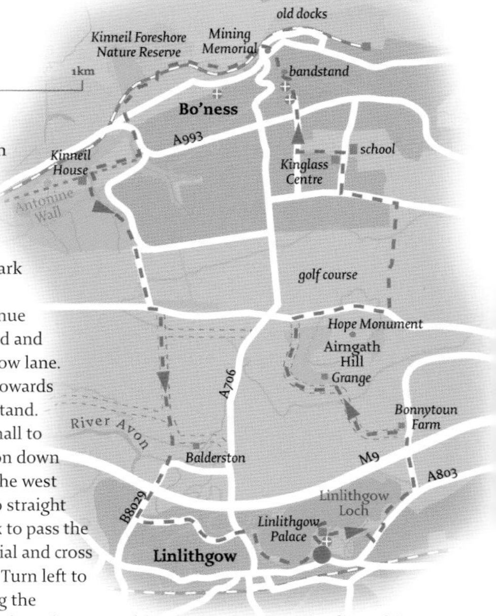

ate at the bottom of
ıe field. The path leads down
ıe edge of the next field to
merge onto a road. Turn
ft and after 400m continue
ownhill at Gauze Road,
ıking a left turn through a park
eyond the Kinglass Centre.

At the end of the path, continue
ownhill to cross the main road and
ırry on to a church and a narrow lane.
t the bottom, cross the park towards
ıe cast-iron Glebe Park Bandstand.
kirt the left side of the town hall to
o down a flight of steps and on down
rovidence Brae, emerging at the west
nd of Bo'ness town centre. Go straight
n across the road and car park to pass the
inding wheel mining memorial and cross
ıe main road and the railway. Turn left to
ıllow the John Muir Way along the
reshore. After returning over the railway,
ırn right to take a path round to a parking
rea and up Snab Lane. The lane continues
n the other side of the A904, heading up to
ıe A993 where you carry on uphill before
ırning right onto Kinneil House driveway.

Go through the gateway on the house's
ft to walk uphill, turning right at the road
ıd left beyond the car park, continuing
ıe climb through the forest. Emerging
om the trees at a crosspaths, turn left past
gateway and carry on uphill, joining the
ad after a gate.

Turn left at the top of the hill with the
ope Monument on its lofty perch ahead.
This commemorates Brigadier Adrian
Hope of Hopetoun House, who was killed
in the Indian Mutiny of 1858 while
attacking the Fort of Roodamow in Oude.
He is buried in Westminster Abbey.

Go right at the next junction to follow
the Public Right of Way to Fishers Brae
straight down the hill. Turn right at the
bottom to walk along the edge of the road
and cross back over the M9 into Linlithgow.

Signs for Linlithgow Link West lead
down Avalon Gardens and Mill Lade. At
the end, cross the A706 and turn left, then
right back to Linlithgow Loch. Go over the
bridge and along the shore to the palace.

Bo'ness to Blackness Castle

Distance **14.8km** Time **3 hours 45**
Terrain **good surfaced paths and unsurfaced forest tracks**
Map **OS Explorer 349** Access **regular bus service to Blackness from Linlithgow**

A wonderful preserved railway and a medieval castle await you on this walk along the shoreline of the Firth of Forth.

The route begins at the winding wheel mining memorial near Bo'ness foreshore. A wander around the town centre just east of it will reveal some interesting architecture, including an ochre-coloured mid-17th-century merchant's house, an 18th-century tobacco warehouse and Scotland's first purpose-built cinema, the art-deco hippodrome. Cross the A904 and the railway track and bear right at the fork to take the path east along the foreshore.

The large yellow buoy by the dock was designed by Isambard Kingdom Brunel some time between 1820 and 1850. Carry on alongside the dock and past the Museum of Scottish Railways. You may find yourself transported back to the steam age on this first section as the whistles of vintage locomotives follow you along the foreshore: the Bo'ness and Kinneil Railway which featured in time-travelling drama *Outlander*, operates from here.

Continue eastwards to wind through woodland. The path passes the Upper Forth Boat Club and follows a concrete walkway just a few metres from the high tide line. A track leads straight ahead, eventually becoming an embankment. Come off this to join a path that runs parallel to it, turning right at a junction to head towards Bridgeness Road.

Cross the road and continue eastwards crossing the road again at the corner. Go

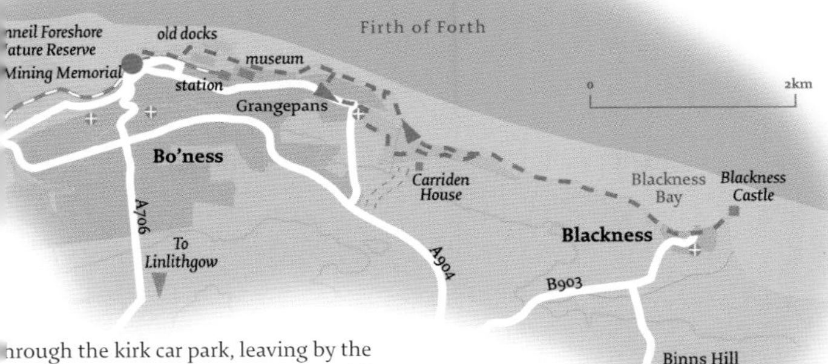

hrough the kirk car park, leaving by the ate to take a wide forest track. Bear right o head uphill and almost immediately eft to enter a field via a gate. The path ontinues eastwards before climbing up he hill across the middle of the field, hen drops gently through the trees to ross a very narrow, high-sided wooden ridge to a junction where you turn left.

At a fork, a short diversion leads to a retty woodland waterfall, but the main oute continues uphill to arrive at a unction by an overgrown gate. Continue astwards along the southern edge of the voods, descending to turn right at the ottom of the hill. The woodland here is nostly elm – known for being very water esistant, this wood was vital to the Bo'ness hipbuilding industry which flourished rom the early 1600s until Victorian times.

Still heading eastwards, emerge from he woods and walk along the shore. Rounding a corner, you can see why lackness Castle is known as 'The Ship hat Never Sailed'. The central tower of he castle is often called the 'main mast' vhile the north and south towers are named the 'stem' and the 'stern'.

Continue along Blackness Bay, through Blackness and on to the castle, also featured in *Outlander* (fee to enter the building itself). Built in the 1440s by Sir George Crichton, Lord High Admiral of Scotland and Sheriff of Linlithgow, it remained in use until the end of the First World War and is now in the care of Historic Scotland.

From the castle, retrace your steps along the shore to the elmwood. Instead of following the outward route back up the hill, continue straight along the shore to pass an old sea gate in around 600m. This was the entrance to the grounds of Burnfoot House and just inside the gate is a plaque to Colonel James Gardiner of Burnfoot who was killed at the Battle of Prestonpans, the first main battle of the 1745 Jacobite Uprising. The ruins of his birthplace are a little way along the shore.

Reaching Bo'ness, the path joins a road as it skirts a boatyard, then turns right to return to the shore and runs parallel to the embankment. Climb up and retrace your steps to the start.

Wester Shore Wood and Midhope Castle

Distance **9.5km** Time **2 hours 30**
Terrain **surfaced and unsurfaced woodland tracks, some minor roads**
Maps **OS Explorer 349 and 350**
Access **regular bus service to Blackness from Linlithgow**

This beautiful woodland walk links the historic castles of Blackness and Midhope. The latter castle, situated in the grounds of Hopetoun House, is not always open to the public due to other estate activities, so check the Hopetoun website before you set off.

The village of Blackness began as a port for Linlithgow at a time when all goods from British colonies had to pass through Britain before proceeding to their intended destination. Growing up around Blackness Castle, it quickly became one of Scotland's most important ports, second only to Leith. Better harbours opened further upriver, however, at Bo'ness and Grangemouth, with easier links to the Forth & Clyde Canal terminus, and Blackness's glory days came to an end.

Head east along the shore from the centre of Blackness, turning right through a metal gate around 80m before the castle. Follow the path up the hill to reach the remains of a chapel which was destroyed by Oliver Cromwell's troops during their siege of 1650. From here, drop downhill towards a ruined doocot, also destroyed in 1650. Scramble down the hill towards the sea and continue eastwards across the grass that fringes the shore before following the Black Burn inland. Cross the burn by a small metal bridge and bear left to follow the track through the trees. Keep left at the next fork.

Eventually the path reaches a junction. (You will return here from Abercorn Church if access to Midhope Castle is restricted.) Follow the path around to the left to cross the Midhope Burn. Turn left

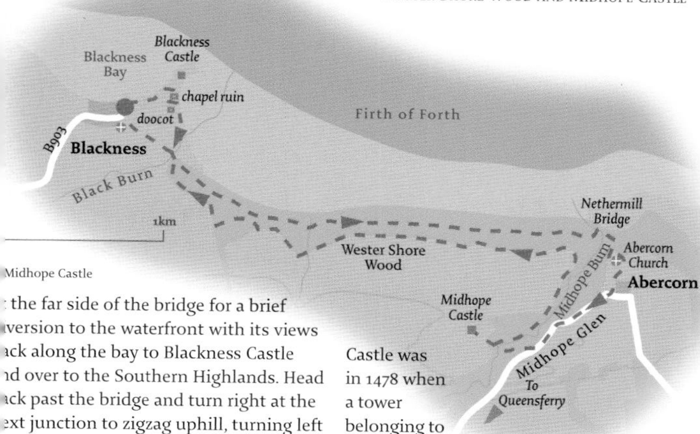

Midhope Castle

: the far side of the bridge for a brief ıversion to the waterfront with its views ıck along the bay to Blackness Castle ıd over to the Southern Highlands. Head ıck past the bridge and turn right at the ext junction to zigzag uphill, turning left the top to swing around and enter the ounds of Abercorn Church.

The size and seclusion of the tiny ımlet of Abercorn belies the site's one-ne importance. A Pictish church stood ere in the late 400s when it was visited St Ninian. Starting life as a two-celled uilding in the mid-12th century, the esent kirk was expanded in 1597 llowing the Reformation and again in 38 and 1893.

If it is not possible to visit Midhope stle, return to the bridge over the dhope Burn, then go left uphill to meet rosspaths by a gate and turn right to gin your return along the southern ge of the wood. Otherwise, go round e kirk and across the graveyard to a gate the top corner. Walk through Abercorn, ning right at the end of the road to low it for 500m. Turn right to head wnhill to the castle (entrance fee).

The earliest known record of Midhope Castle was in 1478 when a tower belonging to the Martin family was situated here. It was remodelled in 1587 by Alexander Drummond and again in 1678 by the Hopes, who would go on to build nearby Hopetoun House a couple of decades later.

Take the track next to the gateway that leads alongside the burn into the woods. The path rises gradually to accompany a drystane dyke, with the burn in a deep and picturesque gorge far below. Go through a metal gate and straight across a crosspaths to follow the forest roads along the southern edge of the wood.

Continue straight ahead at the next junction to follow the path as it swings around to the right, descending gently. Bear left to take a minor track across a footbridge, turning left at the crosspaths to arrive back at the entrance to the woods. Go straight ahead up the grassy track and through a gate at the top of the hill towards Blackness Church, turning right to return to Blackness.

Abercorn to South Queensferry

Distance 14km Time 3 hours 30 Terrain good surfaced paths and unsurfaced tracks Map OS Explorer 350 Access no public transport to Abercorn; buses from Linlithgow and South Queensferry to Newton, leaving a half hour walk to the start point

From an ancient church to an historic port, this walk passes an impressive stately home and beneath all three of the great bridges over the Forth.

Centred on the ancient Abercorn Church, the picturesque hamlet of Abercorn is simply a few houses clustered around a bend in a minor country road. At one end of the hamlet, a little lane leads off to the kirk. Go through the gate at the top end of the wall and zigzag downhill, turning right at the bottom to follow the path through a gate and into Hopetoun Estate. Turn left at a T-junction and follow the estate road for 1km, passing the ruined Staneyhill Tower on the hill. Built around 1630, it was the seat of the Shairps of Staneyhill, Keepers of th King's Purse.

Leaving the estate road at a cottage, go through a gate and continue to a junction. Turn right to head uphill, swinging left to go through another gate. Beyond another cottage, the road becomes a narrow track. Go through another gate, bearing left through an old stone gateway to walk along the top of a rough field. At the far end, take the middle path to turn left onto a surfaced path and follow it all the way downhill, turning right at the bottom to pass beneath the Queensferry Crossing.

This is the newest of the three bridges that span the Forth at South Queensferry

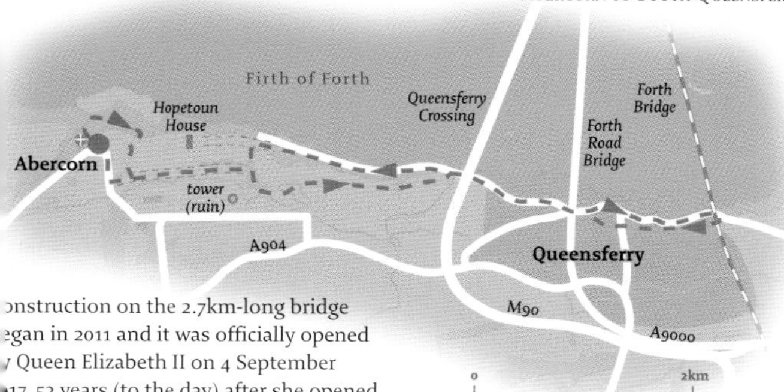

ɔnstruction on the 2.7km-long bridge
ɛgan in 2011 and it was officially opened
/ Queen Elizabeth II on 4 September
•17, 53 years (to the day) after she opened
.e adjacent Forth Road Bridge, which you
ıss under 1km further along the road. At
.e time of its opening in 1964, the Forth
ɔad Bridge was the largest suspension
'idge in the world, replacing the ferry
.at had run between North and South
ɹeensferry for almost 1000 years. It is the
ıly one of the bridges that allows
ːdestrians to cross the Forth.

At the crossroads beneath the bridge,
.rn left to descend into South
ɹeensferry, continuing straight on at the
nction with The Loan to walk along the
ıgh Street. The magnificent Forth Bridge
ɔminates South Queensferry. Designed
' Sir John Fowler and Sir Benjamin
ıker, its 500m cantilever bridge spans
ɛre the longest in the world when it
•ened in 1890. It was voted Scotland's
eatest man-made wonder in 2016 and is
ɔw a UNESCO World Heritage Site.

Pass beneath the Forth Bridge, turning
ʒht just beyond it to climb a long flight
steps up the side of the bridge. At the
p, bear right to follow a long straight
th (the old railway line) that descends
ntly back into the town.

At a car park, climb the steps in the top corner and turn right to follow Morison Gardens back to the crossroads beneath the Road Bridge and out of town. Carry straight on to eventually reach the road that clings to the shore, only leaving it when you reach the impressive Romanesque pillars and wrought-iron gates of the semi-circular gateway to Hopetoun House.

Home to the Marquess of Linlithgow, Hopetoun was built in 1698 but was entirely redesigned by Scottish architect William Adam from 1721 and, following his death in 1748, was completed by his sons, creating Scotland's first Georgian stately home. It was the first major commission for second son Robert Adam who went on to become the most celebrated of Britain's early classical revivalists.

Follow the estate drive as far as a junction where you turn left to go uphill, turning right at the next junction to take the road straight across the Hopetoun Estate and through a gate at the far side. Turn right along the road to return to Abercorn.

he Forth Bridge

Railway walk to Ratho

Distance 9.5km Time 2 hours 30 (one way) Terrain well-defined unsurfaced tracks and surfaced footpaths; one steep flight of steps early in the route, which may be avoided by starting at Dalmeny Station Map OS Explorer 350 Access buses to South Queensferry from Edinburgh and Linlithgow; trains to Dalmeny from Edinburgh; buses operate from Ratho Station back to South Queensferry

Follow the route of the railway that carried the steel used in the construction of the Forth Bridge, passing the site of the first Scottish Parliament on the way.

The railway from Ratho Station to South Queensferry opened in 1866 and was extended in 1878 to run on a steep gradient downhill to the Royal Naval Establishment at Port Edgar. Most, if not all, of the steel for the Forth Bridge was brought to South Queensferry on this line. It closed in 1967.

Starting on the waterfront in South Queensferry, pass beneath the Forth Bridge and turn right to climb the steep 120 steps up the side of the bridge. (This may be avoided by starting at Dalmeny Station instead, heading east along Station Road for 100m to join the path.)

Turn right at the top to go back under the bridge, then left to follow the signs t the station. Descend to the railway path and follow it uphill to pass beneath one of the stone arches at the southern end of the bridge. The alternative start from Dalmeny Station joins the route at the next roadbridge.

After passing beneath the A90, bear right to walk parallel to the railway line, passing through a staggered stone barri and onto a long unsurfaced track, descending a set of steps at the end and passing beneath the railway. Turn left to follow an old road at the side of a field, going through another staggered stone

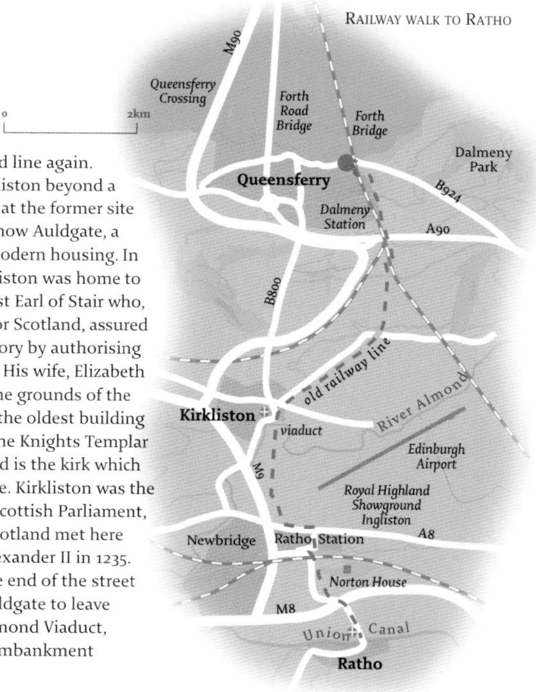

'he Almond Viaduct

ırrier to reach the old line again.
The line enters Kirkliston beyond a
etal barrier to arrive at the former site
Kirkliston Station, now Auldgate, a
sidential street of modern housing. In
e 17th century, Kirkliston was home to
hn Dalrymple, the 1st Earl of Stair who,
Secretary of State for Scotland, assured
mself a place in history by authorising
e Glencoe Massacre. His wife, Elizabeth
ındas, is buried in the grounds of the
rish church. This is the oldest building
the town, built by the Knights Templar
the 12th century, and is the kirk which
ve the town its name. Kirkliston was the
iginal home of the Scottish Parliament,
ıen the Estates of Scotland met here
ıring the reign of Alexander II in 1235.
Cross the road at the end of the street
d carry on down Auldgate to leave
kliston over the Almond Viaduct,
ntinuing along an embankment
oss the fields.
ust before you reach a narrow
otbridge over a road, bear left to descend
the road and go left again to follow it
st some cottages which sit at the end
the runway at Edinburgh Airport. After
gentle serenity of the old railway line
an come as something of a shock when
lane flies over your head!
'urn left to walk along the busy
inburgh Road. Cross the footbridge at
tho Station, turning up Station Road to
low it up and over the railway at the
of the hill. Cross Harvest Wynd and
follow the road uphill, entering the
grounds of the Norton House Hotel and
immediately turning right along a track
that runs through the trees parallel to
Harvest Road.

Bear left to cross the old Norton
Quarry, which operated between the late
19th century and the 1950s. Reaching a
road, turn left to cross the M8 and
descend into Ratho, passing the church to
arrive at a pleasant picnic area beside
Bridge 15 on the Union Canal.

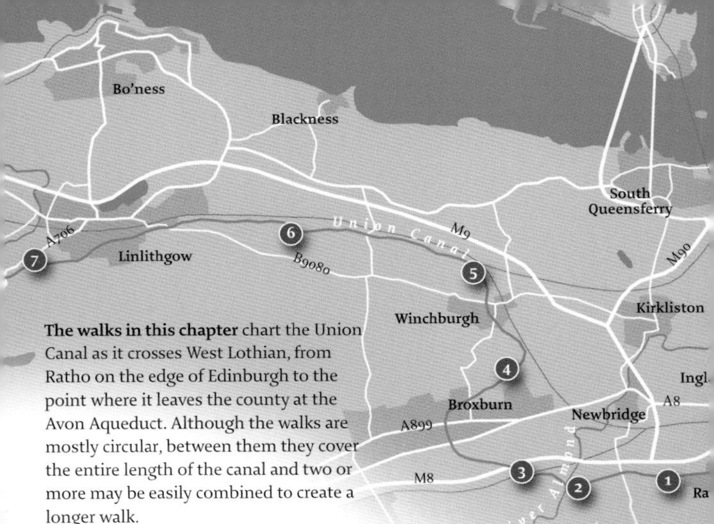

The walks in this chapter chart the Union Canal as it crosses West Lothian, from Ratho on the edge of Edinburgh to the point where it leaves the county at the Avon Aqueduct. Although the walks are mostly circular, between them they cover the entire length of the canal and two or more may be easily combined to create a longer walk.

It wasn't long after the opening of the Forth & Clyde Canal in 1790 that the idea of extending the link to Edinburgh arose, creating the first super-highway between Scotland's two biggest cities. The Edinburgh and Glasgow Union Canal was designed by Hugh Baird and Thomas Telford and opened in 1822 after four years' construction. They managed to create a canal that followed the contours of the land, except for a flight of 11 locks linking the Union Canal with the Forth & Clyde at Falkirk. Where it was not possible to stick to the contours, three great aqueducts were constructed: over the Water of Leith at Slateford, over the Almond near Ratho and over the Avon near Linlithgow. The canal was crossed by 62 bridges, each of them with a number engraved into the keystone.

Although it was initially popular, providing transport for both goods an passengers, when the Edinburgh to Glasgow Railway opened in 1842, trade rapidly and continued to decline stead over the next century.

By the end of the 20th century, howe interest in the canals was growing and Millennium Link Restoration Project began. Bridges replaced the old culver an aqueduct spanned the City Bypass a new bridge was constructed on the M In Edinburgh, a brand-new stretch of canal was dug, along with a terminus. Most impressive of all, the locks at Fal were replaced with the Falkirk Wheel, world's first rotating boat lift, capable moving boats between the two canals under five minutes. The restored cana opened in 2001 and the Falkirk Wheel following year.

Along the Union Canal

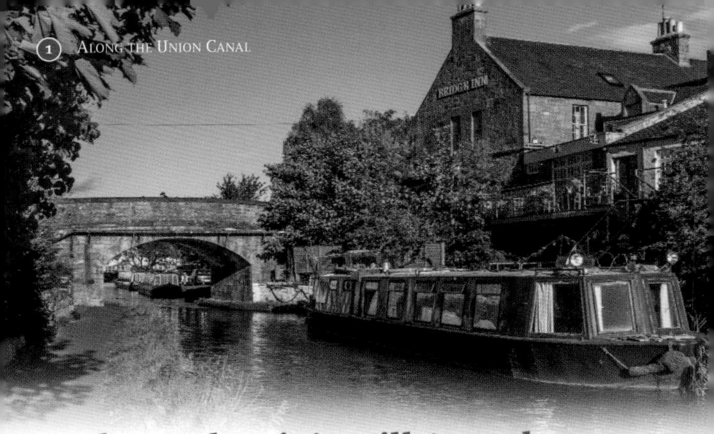

Ratho to the Lin's Mill Aqueduct

Distance **8.4km** Time **2 hours 15**
Terrain **mostly surfaced path, unsurfaced track** Map **OS Explorer 350** Access **regular bus service to Ratho from Livingston and Edinburgh**

When the Union Canal was opened in 1822, it was one of the engineering marvels of the age. Engineer Hugh Baird had designed a route from the centre of Edinburgh to Falkirk along a constant level of 73m above sea level. The entire route of this walk is laid out in a map carved into a statuette at Bridge 15 commemorating the horse-drawn barges that originally worked here. This walk follows the canal to West Lothian's eastern border before returning over Platts Hill.

The route begins in Ratho at the Bridge Inn, an 18th-century farmhouse which was converted into a pub in around 1818 to service the navvies building the canal. Cross the bridge, descend to the towpath and turn right. The headquarters of the Seagull Trust are next to the Bridge Inn. Founded in 1978, the Trust provides cana cruises for disabled people across Scotland. A decorative bench beside the path has a map carved into its back, illustrating how the Union Canal works with the contours of the land.

At Wilkie's Basin the canal widens. The small wooden castle on the island is use in the run-up to Christmas when barges are berthed at the island and Santa greet the children with gifts.

The canal passes over the Bonnington Aqueduct. This replaced the original aqueduct in 1978 when the road below was being widened. During the work, timbers were dredged up in Wilkie's Basi that were thought to be from one of the original 'Swift' canal boats. When these were introduced in 1822, they cut the journey time between Edinburgh and Glasgow from 12 uncomfortable hours b

'he Bridge Inn

agecoach to eight hours of smooth iling. The Swifts did not last long, owever, as the opening of the Edinburgh d Glasgow Railway in 1842 cut the urney time to two hours.

Beyond Bridge 18, the canal rounds a rner; you can see the canal feeder owing into the Lin's Mill Basin with the n's Mill Aqueduct immediately ahead. sing some 23m above the River Almond, is is the third highest aqueduct in itain and it is worth taking a short version across it to admire the view wn to the Almond Valley Viaduct.

Returning to the eastern end of the ueduct, turn left through a gap in the ll – signposted for the country park – descend, passing beneath the archway d heading straight up to the end of the ad, where it meets with the corner of other road. Continue straight on here. Pass the cottages at Clifton Mains, cross dge 16 and go past Clifton Hall School.

The estate at Clifton dates to the 1240s, but the present mansion was built in 1857 and it became a private boarding school in 1930. Reaching a junction, cross the road and continue up the path signposted Ratho Paths Network. Bear left to walk along the edge of a field, following a sign for Ratho via Platts Hill.

Cross a large gravel area to follow the road up the hill past the Edinburgh International Climbing Arena. Opened in 2003, the building is home to the largest indoor climbing wall in the world.

Continue past some boulders and go straight ahead at the next junction to pass a metal gate which leads into woodland. There are a few buildings dotted around as the road reaches the outskirts of Ratho before descending to meet with Baird Road. Turn to the right and head down the hill, passing the church and crossing the bridge to return to the Bridge Inn.

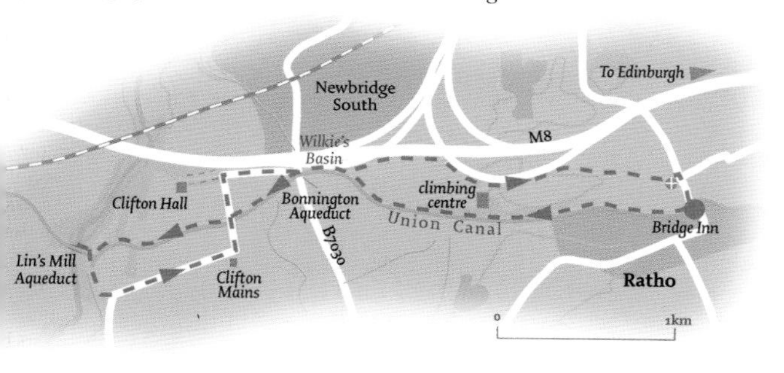

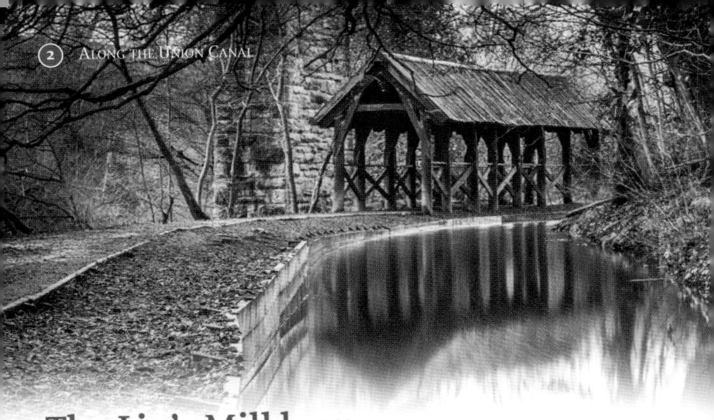

The Lin's Mill loop

Distance 10.9km Time 2 hours 45 Terrain good footpaths, some surfaced; some of the later stages are on minor roads Map OS Explorer 350 Access regular bus service to Mid Calder from Livingston and Edinburgh

Almondell sits in the former grounds of Almondell House, built in 1789 by Lord Advocate Henry Erskine. Erskine planted many of the trees and shrubs in the park himself. He was friends with Robert Burns, a frequent visitor to Almondell, who made Erskine the subject of his poem 'The Dean of the Faculty'. This (mainly) riverbank walk follows the Union Canal's water supply from its source to its link with the canal at the Lin's Mill Aqueduct.

Follow the signs for the visitor centre from Almondell's Mid Calder car park. The path crosses a bridge, climbs a steep hill and drops gently to follow the banks of the River Almond. As you cross a modern bridge you get your first sight of the canal feeder, built between 1818 and 182 as it leaves the Almond just upstream.

Go through what looks rather like an elongated church porch underneath the Camps Viaduct. This curious structure was erected to protect walkers from any potential debris falling from above whe the viaduct was being restored in 1997.

The unusual bridge to the right is the Canal Feeder Aqueduct. Built in 1820, it was designed by Hugh Baird and Thom Telford, who were also responsible for t Union Canal itself.

Cross the aqueduct and turn left to w past a wildflower meadow. Go straight across a larger path, climbing the hill to join a tree-lined walkway on the very ec of the park before dropping to the river At the bottom, turn right, and follow tl footpath along the canal feeder.

After a series of gates and stiles, the privately-owned Illieston Castle, a favourite royal hunting seat of James II

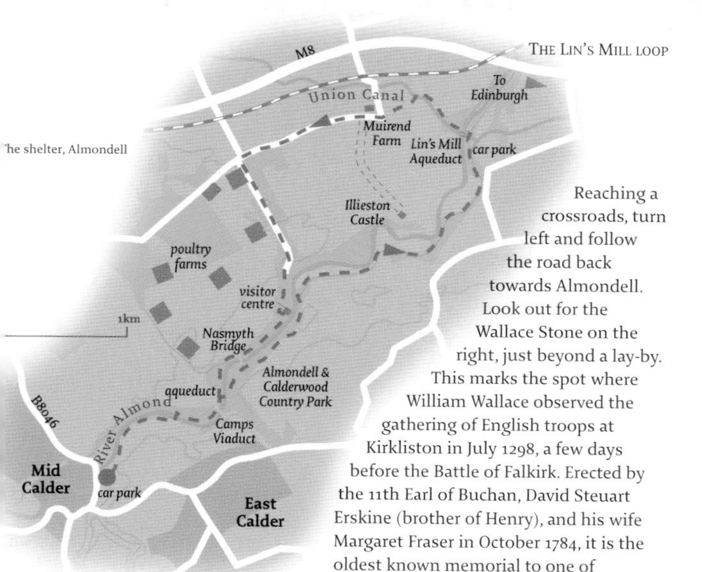

'he shelter, Almondell

d James IV, appears on the left. At the
of a set of steps, turn left onto a very
nor road, then fork right to reach the
ion Canal car park.

'he Lin's Mill Aqueduct, completed in
:2 and named after the nearby 17th-
ıtury cornmill once owned by William
, crosses the deep wooded gorge of
River Almond in five arches, some
n above the river. Lin was the last
son in Scotland to die of the plague.
; wife had to bury him herself after she
s refused help.

;o down the steps beside the aqueduct
l up the other side, turning right to
ss it. Leave the towpath at the first exit,
ssing Bridge 19 and continuing along a
n road before joining a minor road at
irend Farm.

Reaching a crossroads, turn left and follow the road back towards Almondell. Look out for the Wallace Stone on the right, just beyond a lay-by. This marks the spot where William Wallace observed the gathering of English troops at Kirkliston in July 1298, a few days before the Battle of Falkirk. Erected by the 11th Earl of Buchan, David Steuart Erskine (brother of Henry), and his wife Margaret Fraser in October 1784, it is the oldest known memorial to one of Scotland's great national heroes.

Follow the road through the gateway back into Almondell and head towards the visitor centre, passing beneath a banner representing Uranus, part of the Kirkhill Pillar Project. This celebrates the work of David Steuart Erskine, who built a scale model of the solar system in his garden at Kirkhill in Broxburn. The pillar now sits in front of the visitor centre.

Take the path to the left of the visitor centre, turning right along the riverbank. Look out for the Fraser Stone on the left, by a bridge. This was also erected by Margaret Fraser, this time in memory of her ancestor Sir Simon Fraser, who fought with Wallace in the fight for independence.

Walk along the riverbank to the Canal Feeder Aqueduct and return to the start.

Lin's Mill to Broxburn

Distance 7.9km Time 2 hours
Terrain canal towpath, surfaced paths, country roads, unsurfaced track
Map OS Explorer 350 Access no public transport to Lin's Mill

West Lothian is often referred to as 'Corridor County': the old canal, the Edinburgh to Glasgow railway line, the modern M8 and the trunk road of the A89 all enter the county in the east and leave again in the west. On this walk you follow the oldest of these, the Union Canal, as it enters West Lothian at the Lin's Mill Aqueduct before meandering northwards towards Broxburn.

The route begins at the canal basin at the Lin's Mill Aqueduct. What is now the car park at Lin's Mill was formerly a busy wharf where lime produced at Camps near East Calder was brought by horse and cart, loaded onto canal barges and taken on to Edinburgh or to the iron and steelworks at Airdrie and Coatbridge.

Go down the steps beside the aquedu and up the other side to cross it and continue along the towpath. Further on, the canal dogtails beneath the modern Bridge 21A which carries the M8 over it. When the M8 was constructed in the 1960s and '70s, it simply blocked the rou of the canal. The bridge was built in 200 signified by the MM inscription, as part the Millennium Link restoration project The opening of the new bridge was celebrated when boats from Linlithgow and Ratho met bow to bow.

A little way on, you'll see a curious building attached to Bridge 23: this was used to store food for the horses that pulled the barges along the canal. The eyelet in the wall provided ventilation. There were originally stables here too, b they seem to have been demolished by 1897. The canal opens in a winding hole just before the bridge. A piece of artwor

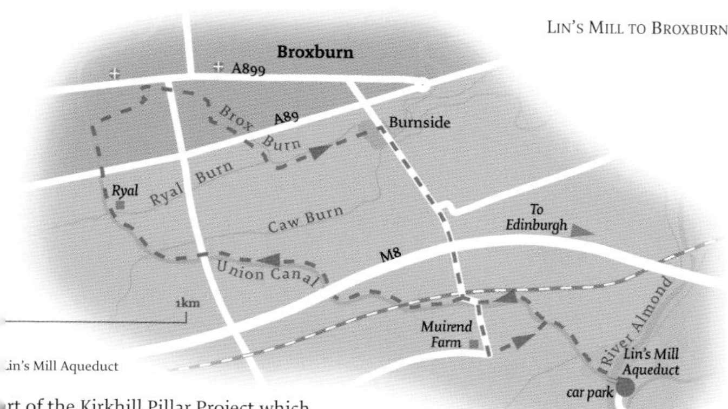

ˌin's Mill Aqueduct

ırt of the Kirkhill Pillar Project which lebrates the work of mathematician ıvid Steuart Erskine, 11th Earl of Buchan, ıd representing Saturn, is attached to e far pillar of the bridge.

On the outskirts of Broxburn, the red-ick and iron Holygate South Road idge carries the A89 Broxburn bypass ross the canal, the girders on its ıderside home to hundreds of nesting geons. When it was built in the 1930s, e bridge was designed to carry a light lway alongside the A89, but the railway ıs never constructed.

There are houses on both sides of the ıal as it enters Broxburn, but they are up an embankment and the route still ls surprisingly rural. Look out for an oak am topped with a model of the planet ɔiter, another artwork from the Kirkhill lar Project, on the opposite bank.

Climb the steps immediately after dge 25 and turn left, following the sign the Brox Burn Path. The path parallels towpath for a while before suddenly ning right to enter a housing estate. ntinue straight ahead, crossing a road and a footbridge over the Brox Burn, which gives the town its name. Turn hard right, to walk along the road. Cross Station Road and continue straight ahead again, turning right onto Hall Road. Bear left at the fork and left again after crossing the burn to follow the path to the busy A89.

Cross with great care and walk along a farm track signposted 'Public Path'. Just before a gate, a narrow track leads left, still following the course of the Brox Burn. The track becomes a wide leafy street in the attractive little hamlet of Burnside. At the end of the road, turn right onto a minor country road and follow it up the hill towards Muirend. The road crosses the M8 before going underneath the railway. Rather than rejoin the towpath, cross Bridge 20 when you reach it and climb uphill.

Go through the gate on the corner by Muirend Farm and follow the track, crossing Bridge 19 before following the towpath back to Lin's Mill.

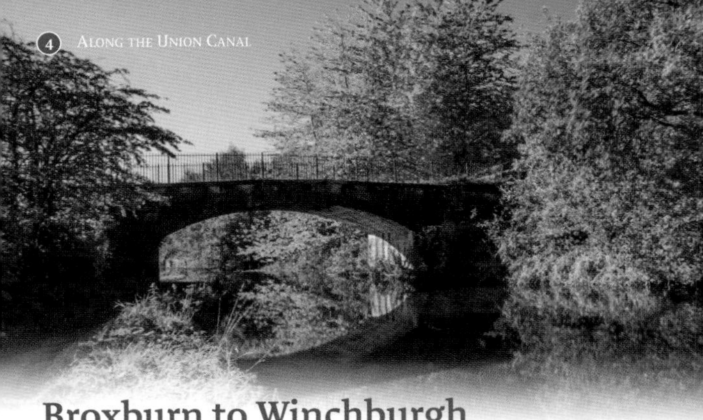

Broxburn to Winchburgh

Distance 9.4km Time 2 hours 30 Terrain surfaced footpaths, grassy track Map OS Explorer 350 Access regular bus service to Broxburn from Livingston and Linlithgow

In the Union Canal's heyday, coal from West Lothian's mines was transported east to fuel Edinburgh's many fires. The barges returned laden with horse dung and nightsoil from the city, which the farmers of West Lothian bought to grow their crops. As part of an original 'circular economy', these in turn were shipped by canal to the markets in the city. This walk takes you through West Lothian's former industrial heartlands, returning via a 16th-century towerhouse.

The headquarters of the Bridge 19-40 Union Canal Society, a voluntary organisation which maintains the canal between the Lin's Mill Aqueduct and Philpstoun, are situated at Port Buchan in Broxburn. Broxburn's cargo-handling facilities were situated at this small canal basin. Start by the Canal Society building in Broxburn and walk up to Mai Street. Cross the road and down to the towpath, then pass under the bridge to head north, passing Port Buchan opposi

Beyond Bridge 27 Greendykes Bing comes into view and by the time you ha passed Bridge 29 it towers imposingly above the opposite bank. This huge bin is a scheduled historic monument to th industry that created it. At 95m high, it i the largest of West Lothian's bings and, according to some estimates, it contain 15 million tonnes of spoil, which would make it one of the heaviest man-made objects on the planet!

Presently the canal passes beneath Bridge 30, with Niddry Castle dwarfed b Niddry Bing on the right. On the outski of Winchburgh, the canal enters a deep cutting, with the trees forming a canop across the water.

Climb the steps immediately after

Bridge 29, Easter Mains Bridge

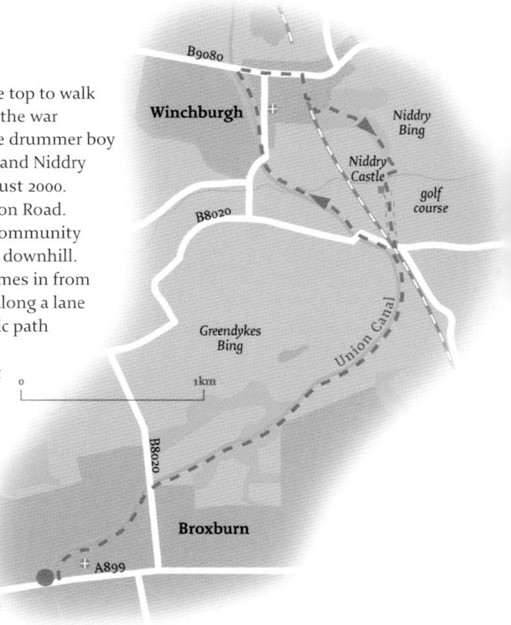

:idge 32, turning left at the top to walk ong Main Street and pass the war .emorial, a statue of a little drummer boy ected by the Winchburgh and Niddry oyal British Legion in August 2000. Cross Main Street at Station Road. ut through Winchburgh Community arden and follow the path downhill. pproaching a road that comes in from e right, bear left to head along a lane id turn right down a public path etween two fences at the de of the railway. Turn left the end. At the first orner, a track leads off ross rough grassland id swings towards iddry Bing. Just as the ith begins to climb its wer slopes, turn right to llow another track that sappears into woodland. Niddry Castle Golf Course through the trees to the ght. It was formerly the site of Niddry astle Oil Works, constructed in 1902 to ocess shale dug from beneath the opetoun Estate. The works closed in 1960 id Niddry Bing is all that remains. nerging onto the golf course, turn right walk along the edge of the burn. Cross the bridge to climb the steps up to iddry Castle. The castle was built around 90 by the Seton family, and was the ome of Mary Seton, one of Mary, Queen Scots' ladies-in-waiting. Queen Mary herself stayed here in May 1568 following her escape from Loch Leven Castle, before defeat at the Battle of Langside forced her final flight to England, captivity and execution. The castle was sold to the Hope family in around 1680 and became part of the Hopetoun Estate but fell into disrepair in the early 1700s. It was restored in the 1990s and is now a private residence.

Go down the drive, turning right to cross the railway and follow the canal towpath back to Broxburn.

Winchburgh to Fawnspark

Distance 8.9km Time 2 hours 15
Terrain easy canal towpath, woodland tracks, surfaced paths and roads
Maps OS Explorer 349 and 350
Access regular bus service to Winchburgh from Livingston and Linlithgow

This is a walk of two halves, a pleasant stroll along the canal towpath, returning along an informal woodland track.

Beginning where the canal passes underneath Winchburgh Main Street, go down to the towpath and continue north. Almost immediately, the bustle of Winchburgh is left behind. After the canal goes beneath Bridge 33, it widens out into a canal basin before entering a bright and airy passage through oak, sycamore, elm and beech woodland.

Eventually, the canal enters a shallow cutting and the trees that project across the canal form an enclosed green tunnel. An attractive stone bench is built into the dyke that lines the cutting.

Look out for kicking stones – large stones embedded along the edge of the towpath to warn horses that they were getting too near the edge – in the stretch between Bridges 36 and 37.

Turning a corner, Philpstoun Bing comes into sight. Fawnspark farmhouse is on the opposite side of the canal. Turn right at the car park at Fawnspark and immediately right again to take the path into the woodland. The track sticks closely to the line of the towpath, just a few metres below you through the trees.

Cross Bridge 37 and follow the track through the trees, going over a farm track and swinging left after 400m to continue

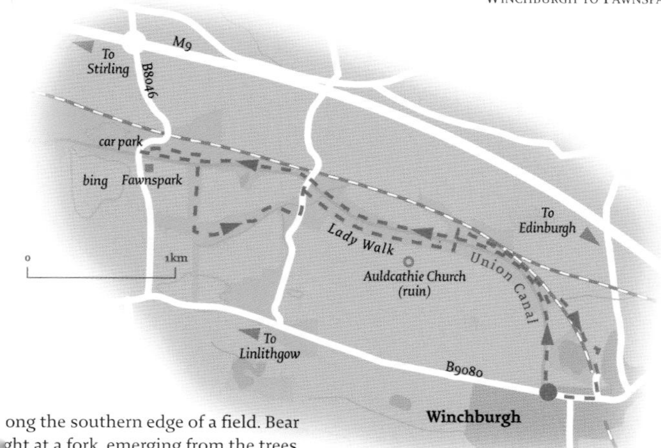

ong the southern edge of a field. Bear ght at a fork, emerging from the trees ıto a shrubland of long grass, broom and few small conifers, and follow the track ntil it meets a road. Turn left along the ɔad, going right at a lay-by after 200m follow a woodland track known as ıdy Walk. Soon this reaches the southern lge of the woods.

The ruins of Auldcathie Church can be :en in the nearby field. The church is rst mentioned in records in 1198, when was granted to a William Gifford by ıe Prior of St Andrews. In 1528, one of ıe first martyrs of the Reformation, ɔung, newlywed Patrick Hamilton of ngscavil, was burnt at the stake here. ıe church could not recruit a minister r Auldcathie following the Reformation, ıd stand-ins were sent out from the :arby parishes of Abercorn and 'amond. The Commissioners of ırliament annexed the Parish of ıldcathie to the Parish of Dalmeny in 1618, and Auldcathie Church fell into ruin soon after.

Reaching a more formal path, turn left to cross the canal over Bridge 34, but leave the path just after the bridge to follow a track up a short but steep hill. Turn right at the top and bear right at the next two forks to reach a junction with an overgrown path. Cross the railway and immediately turn right through an open field. Follow the path into a housing estate. Continue straight ahead at the road, turning right and immediately left again. At the top of the hill, a track leads off on the right to pass through a gap by a wall into a field.

Cross the field, following the track through a gap in the fence at the far end to join Station Road. Return to Winchburgh Main Street and follow it west back to the start of the walk.

Ruins of Auldcathie Church

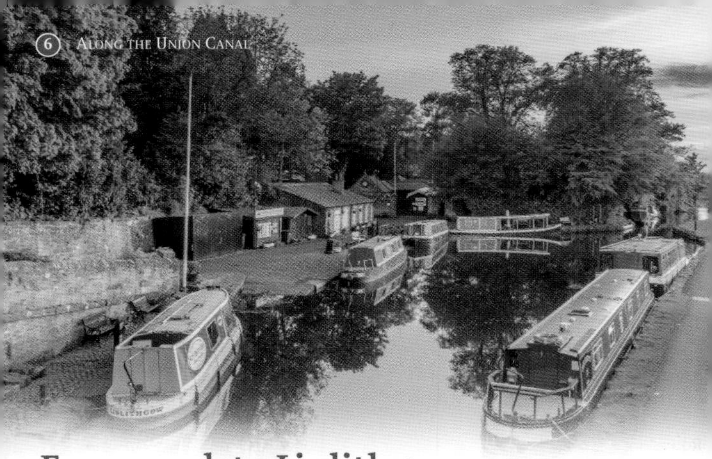

Fawnspark to Linlithgow

Distance **6.3km** Time **1 hour 45 (one way)**
Terrain **surfaced canal towpath throughout** Map **OS Explorer 349**
Access **no public transport to Fawnspark; bus back to Philpstoun from Linlithgow**

Leave West Lothian's former industrial heartlands behind and travel through gently rolling countryside to the centre of historic Linlithgow. This is an excellent place to stop for refreshments, or a picnic on the peel beside the loch, before retracing your steps.

Beginning at the car park at Fawnspark, pass beneath Bridge 38. Philpstoun Bing, the last of the great bings that the canal has passed since Broxburn, rises dramatically on both sides of the canal.

There are, in fact, two bings here, known as the North and South Bings, separated by the canal. It is hard to imagine now, but when this section of the canal was built, it flowed across a causeway over Philpstoun Loch. The North Bing grew from the 1880s when Philpstoun Oil Works began production, tipping spent shale waste into the loch north of the canal. By 1914, the North Bir was no longer in use and a new bing was rising out of the water on the southern side of the causeway.

The oil works closed in 1931, leaving these shale bings as surviving evidence (the industry. These days, the bings are scheduled monuments and have becom a haven for wildlife such as foxes, hares, red grouse, badgers, skylarks and common blue butterflies. On the bank opposite the towpath, mature beech, hawthorn and elm are growing up the embankment. A couple of large concrete abutments are the remains of the bridge that carried a tramway up a steep incline taking shale waste to the South Bing.

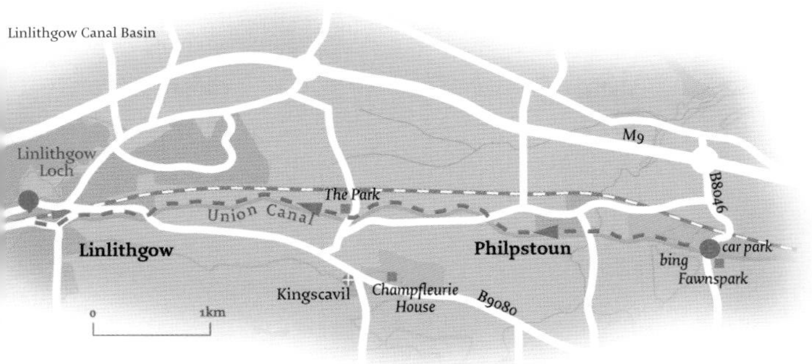

Rounding a corner, Bridge 39, which ,as built in 1820 to allow access to the ields to the north of the canal, comes ıto sight – the platform was levelled in he 1880s to carry a mineral railway.

little way on, the canal enters gentle ırmland. A few rows of houses with their ack gardens facing onto the canal are the nly clue that you are passing Philpstoun.

There is a fine view of the House of the inns and Binns Folly at Bridge 40. Soon he canal arrives at a winding hole, ınding stage and the former stables at ingscavil Park, now a restaurant. The ridge here leads to the hamlet of ingscavil, meaning 'The King's plot of ınd', though it was owned by the Iamiltons. Legend has it that the estate ,as named Champfleurie by Mary, Queen f Scots who, on a picnic there, remarked 'C'est un vrai champfleuri!' ('It is truly a ield of flowers!'). Bonnie Prince Charlie lept in Champfleurie House on his way to ictories at Edinburgh and Prestonpans.

A little further along, another pair of stone abutments carried a private railway from the oil works at Bridgend to join the Edinburgh to Glasgow Line by Linlithgow Station. The railway opened in 1885, but the oil works were destroyed by fire in 1902 and the railway closed the year after.

The large pagoda-like structure on the right as you enter Linlithgow is the former St Magdalene's Distillery, now converted to flats. At one time, this part of the town held a fair and a hospice both named after St Magdalene. Pass beneath Bridge 43 to arrive at Linlithgow Canal Basin. The former stables here are now home to the Linlithgow Union Canal Society, which maintains the canal between Philpstoun and the Avon Aqueduct.

Continue along the towpath to descend a set of steps and turn left onto Strawberry Bank. Go down another set of steps to pass below the railway and down Court Square to the High Street, turning right to head for the Cross, the beautifully ornate well in front of the palace, and the end of the walk.

The Avon Aqueduct circuit

Distance **11.3km** Time **3 hours**
Terrain **good surfaced paths and unsurfaced woodland tracks**
Map **OS Explorer 349** Access **regular bus and rail services to Linlithgow**

At 250m in length, the Avon Aqueduct is the longest aqueduct in Scotland and the second longest in Britain. Built to a design by Hugh Baird with advice from Thomas Telford, its 12 arches carry the canal an airy 26m above the River Avon. This walk follows the canal from Linlithgow to the River Avon, which marks the boundary between West Lothian and Falkirk.

The walk begins at the Canal Basin in Linlithgow. Originally a coal depot and now the home of the Linlithgow Canal Centre it began as two cottages and two stables for four horses. The iron pillar by the tearoom is the remains of an old crane.

Head west along the canal to pass underneath Bridge 44. Just beyond the bridge, the canal widens for a winding hole, used to turn boats around. Already, there is a rural feel to the route but Linlithgow itself is only behind the trees and you can just make out the spire of St Ninian's through the gaps.

Bear left to pass underneath the modern Bridge 45. The narrow width of the original 1820 humpback Bridge 45 was considered too dangerous for traffic going to and from the newly built houses further up Preston Road and it was demolished and replaced with a culvert in 1965, following the closure of the canal. This was replaced again in 1992.

After Bridge 47, incorrectly numbered as 45 on one side, the canal runs alongside the A706 to reach the Woodcockdale Cottages and Stables.

This A-listed building, constructed, like the rest of the canal, in around 1820, would have once provided stables for the horses that worked the towpath. Bear left

Avon Aqueduct

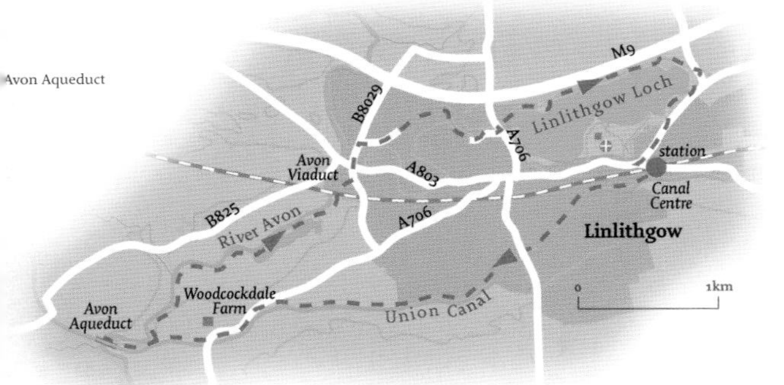

pass underneath Bridge 48. The canal vings to the right and comes quite ıddenly to the Avon Aqueduct.

The view north from the centre of the ɿueduct is spectacular: below, the river ıakes towards the Avon Viaduct and stant Airngath Hill, with the Hope onument prominent on its summit. eturning to the eastern end of the ɿueduct, continue back along the wpath, going down a set of steps at a gnpost to drop towards the River Avon.

Bear left to follow the riverbank north, ıssing the site of the Battle of Linlithgow ridge, which took place here in 1526. The ıttle was the result of an attempt by argaret Tudor, the sister of King Henry III of England and widowed wife of King mes IV of Scotland, to free her young n, James V of Scotland, from the clutches his stepfather, Archibald Douglas, 6th ırl of Angus. The Earl of Lennox, who was ghting for Margaret, crossed the river at a rd here, but was defeated by troops loyal Angus, with many of his men killed ong the banks of the Avon.

The route reaches the Avon Viaduct soon after. Built between 1839 and 1841, its 23 arches, some up to 26m high, straddle the boundary between West Lothian and Falkirk. Continue under the viaduct and back into Linlithgow.

Go through a gate, turning right to walk up Burgh Mills Lane, then follow Mill Road downhill, going straight over the crossroads and turning right onto Justinhaugh Drive. Cross the play area and take a path between the houses in the left corner. Cross a footbridge and bear left to cross a playing field. Turn right onto Avalon Gardens and follow the signs for Linlithgow Link, walking up Lade Court. When you reach the main A706, cross the road and turn left, then right to access Linlithgow Loch.

Bear left at the fork to take the path around the north shore, turning through the gate at the far end to cross Fiddler's Croft to Blackness Road. Head along this towards the town centre. Turn left at the roundabout to go under the railway and follow the path uphill to the canal basin.

Sandwiched between the rumbling M8 and the M9 motorways, the hilly heartlands of West Lothian are a hidden gem. The Bathgate and Riccarton Hills are contiguous ranges of hills connected to the outside world by narrow, twisting roads. Ancient inhabitants found uses for these hills and a prehistoric stone circle crowns Cairnpapple, while there are Iron Age hillforts on Cockleroy and Bowden Hill.

Geologically, the range comprises mostly ash and lava piled up by volcanic activity during the Carboniferous era. The hard-wearing igneous rock has been quarried for stones used in roadbuilding while a vein in the rock produced lead and silver. Meanwhile, sandstone from Binny Quarry at the eastern end of the range was used in some of Edinburgh's grandest buildings, and they were held together with mortar made from lime processed from limestone quarried across the hills. The lime was also used as a fertiliser.

Quarrying has provided new habitats for wildlife, which is being allowed to take over now that the digging has ceased. Sheep and cattle graze contented on the upper hills, while larger fields lower down provide animal feed crops. Badgers and other wildlife live in the tree belts and plantations that shelter these fields and deer hide among the conifer woodlands.

The hills are best enjoyed from Beecraigs Country Park, which grew up around the reservoir built during World War One to provide water for Linlithgow. Beecraigs Forest was originally planted to provide pitprops for West Lothian's burgeoning mining industry, but these days it is enjoyed by walkers, cyclists and horse riders.

The sun sets over Cockleroy Hill

Beecraigs and the Bathgate Hills

Hillhouse Woodland

Distance 2.5km Time 45 minutes Terrain some surfaced paths, mostly woodland tracks; the site is on a hillside and there are some steep climbs Map OS Explorer 349 Access no direct public transport; Beecraigs can be reached from Linlithgow via Preston Road along a traffic-free footpath

Beecraigs Country Park is mostly coniferous woodland but Hillhouse Woodland on the park's northern edge was planted in the late 1990s as mostly mixed broadleaf. Trees such as oak, apple, birch and beech, and bushes of raspberry and bramble, now grow in an area which was formerly farmland. This hillside walk amply rewards the effort with great views.

The walk starts at Beecraigs Visitor Centre and follows the green waymarker around the site. In the past, this area was mined for limestone to produce quicklim for use as a fertiliser, and the remains of the quarries and cave systems are still present among the trees. Today, these are home to Daubenton's and brown long-eared bats. Wildflowers that grow on the grass slopes during summer include the common spotted orchid and wild pansy, and these attract ringlet and small tortoiseshell butterflies amongst others. The area is also abundant with squirrels, rabbits, roe deer and badger.

From the entrance, head round the bac of the visitor centre before following the path through the trees to reach a basket on a pole. This was one of a series of

acons which were lit across the UK on April 2016 to mark the 90th birthday of ueen Elizabeth II.

Cross the road, go through a gate and rn left into the trees. Take a left turn at e next junction, then a sharp right wnhill, following the sign for Hillhouse d Linlithgow.

A track leads off at a waymarker before aring right to reach a clearing and a nch, with views out to the west towards rling. After a level stretch, you come to -junction: head downhill, cutting oss a path and over the grass to other bench with a superb panorama to angemouth, Stirling Castle and the ghlands in the northwest and, heading st, the Ochils, Binns Folly, Rosyth, unfermline, the bridges and beyond.

From this viewpoint, turn left to head west back to the path and continue downhill to skirt around a gateway. Follow the waymarker along a wide grassy path and up a narrow track, forking right to climb steeply back uphill. It's a short but arduous climb, and there is a single wooden seat for resting at the junction at the top of the track.

Continue uphill to cross a clearing, before climbing again to reach an ornamental stone bench with views to Greendykes Bing, Binny Craig, with the Pentlands in the background, Bass Rock, Arthur's Seat, Broomy Knowe and Beecraigs Hill.

Follow the track back to the entrance gate. Cross the road, and head back past the beacon to the visitor centre.

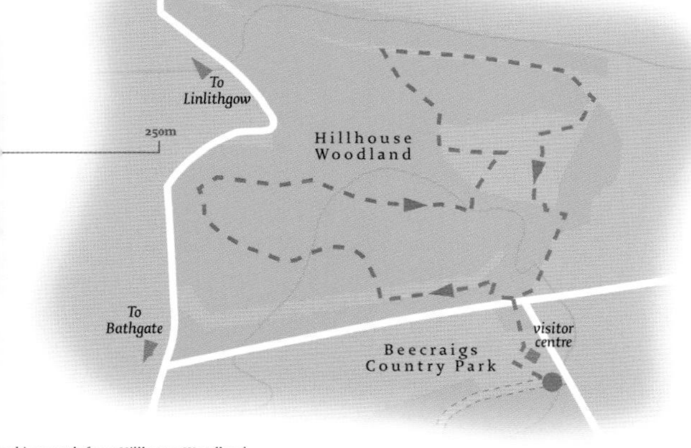

ooking north from Hillhouse Woodland

Beecraigs Loch and Cockleroy

Distance **7.2km** **Time** **2 hours**
Terrain **surfaced paths, unsurfaced woodland tracks, mostly flat except for an optional short climb up the grassy slopes of Cockleroy Hill**
Map **OS Explorer 349** **Access** **no direct public transport; Beecraigs can be reached from Linlithgow via Preston Road along a traffic-free footpath**

Cockleroy means 'Hat of the Kings' which some sources say refers to Linlithgow's status as a Royal Burgh. This walk explores the popular Beecraigs Country Park before enjoying the spectacular views from the summit.

Beginning at Beecraigs Visitor Centre, head downhill on the roadside path, turning left to the animal attractions at the crossroads and crossing the viewing platform. Beecraigs is a working farm and its animals include a herd of red deer, Highland cattle, Belted Galloways and seven different breeds of native Scottish sheep. From the bottom of the viewing platform, continue down the hill, following the orange waymarkers to cross the dam at the end of Beecraigs Loch.

At the start of the First World War, 150 captured German troops were enlisted to dam the Riccarton Burn. Plans were submitted to expand the workforce, but the prisoners were generally unwilling to work and their labour was withdrawn in September 1917. Finally completed by a team of navvies from a camp at Riccarton Mill, the reservoir supplied water to Linlithgow for more than half

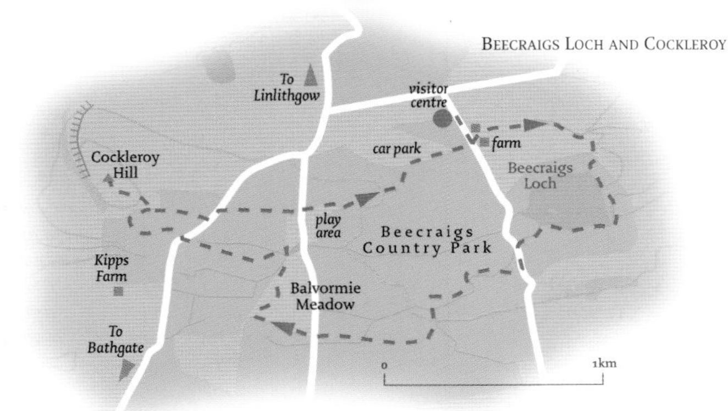

:entury, before being decommissioned 1972 in favour of Loch Lomond.

Descending from the dam and passing e old trout farm, walk gently uphill past ishing lodge and a jetty to cross a ncrete bridge and turn left into the rest. The path shadows the road for a tle before crossing and climbing uphill. ill following the orange waymarkers, go rectly over a staggered crosspaths and rough a gap in a wall.

Bear left to cross a bridge, turning left ;ain to follow the track over a crossroads ıd across a road. Turn right at the nction at the end of the road and bear ;ht to pass Balvormie Meadow which is azed by Beecraigs' cattle and sheep in e autumn. This 'conservation grazing' ops scrub encroaching and increases the eadow's biodiversity.

Now following the blue waymarkers, ·ar right, passing a barbecue area to rive at a toilet block. A plaque on the all of the building, marked 'Could Be', part of the Kirkhill Pillar Project, presenting the planet Pluto.

Turn left here to follow the path gently uphill, crossing a stile and a road and continuing to climb. Over to the left, on the opposite hillside, are the ruins of Kipps Castle, former home to the physician, geographer and natural historian, Sir Robert Sibbald. He was the first Professor of Medicine at the University of Edinburgh, physician to King James VII and co-founder of Scotland's first 'physic garden'.

Bear left at a fork for a fine view of Lochcote Reservoir, then swing around to reach a gate. Climb the short grassy track to the top of Cockleroy Hill. There is a trig point here with a viewing disc detailing the landmarks you can see at every turn. The remains of an Iron Age hillfort are visible along the summit.

Return to the gate at the bottom of the hill, and turn left to follow a long straight track, bearing right to cross the road and then left to follow the sign for Balvormie Play Area. Cross a road and skirt around the play area, turning left to join a wide, pleasant walkway through an avenue of trees that returns you to the visitor centre.

:ishing dinghies on Beecraigs Loch

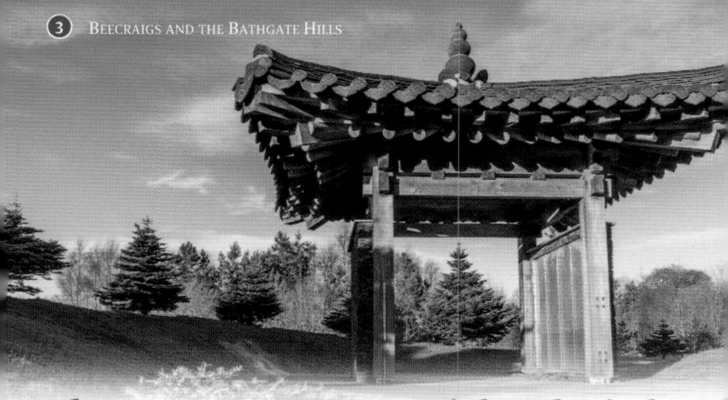

The Korean War Memorial and Witchcrai

Distance 6km Time 1 hour 30
Terrain surfaced paths, steep and muddy hillside and woodland tracks
Map OS Explorer 349 Access there is no public transport to the memorial

The Korean War began when North Korea, with the support of China and the Soviet Union, invaded South Korea in June 1950. The UN and the United States supported South Korea and the three-year conflict, in which millions of Korean civilians died, also claimed the lives of more than 1000 British servicemen. Their names are listed on boards within the traditional Korean-style wood- and slate-crafted pagoda. This walk climbs from the memorial to a medieval Refuge Stone before exploring the southern woodland of Beecraigs Country Park.

The walk begins at the lay-by for the memorial. The pagoda sits between two mounds landscaped in the shape of the Ying and Yang of the Korean flag and planted with 110 Korean firs, one for every 10 men who perished. Surroundin this is an arboretum of 1114 native Scottish trees.

Enter the memorial garden and follow Colonel Johnstone Walk to pass beneat the pagoda, continuing uphill to reach a gate. Carry straight on uphill to reach a circular stone enclosure.

This is the Witchcraig Wall, built in 20 to provide a shelter for walkers. The design was selected to fit in with the drystane dykes of the area, reflecting its historical and agricultural heritage. Although it is primarily constructed fro 400-million-year-old Perthshire sandstones, there are also 43 rocks from Scotland's Central Belt randomly placed within the wall, chosen to represent the landscape visible from this vantage poi

Built into the dyke behind the Witchcraig Wall is a medieval Refuge Stone, with the Cross of Lorraine carved into its surface. This stone was one of t

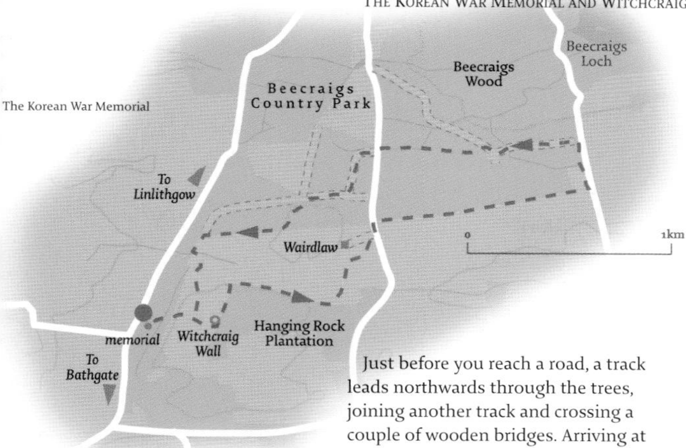

oundary stones that formed a one-mile rcle around Torphichen Preceptory. he area within the circle offered a legal nctuary, or refuge, to every criminal or ebtor who entered its precincts and mained there.

Returning to the Witchcraig Wall, ead north along a track down the hill. round halfway down, cross a stile on e right and follow the track eastwards. his mixed broadleaf and conifer oodland provides a habitat capable of pporting numerous species – badgers d rabbits thrive here and kestrels have so been sighted. Most of the trees were anted in the 1990s, but there are also ature specimens.

Follow the white waymarkers downhill, rough a gap in the fence and back uphill briefly follow a minor road. Turn right at sign for Beecraigs onto Guthrie's Path, an d drove road which runs along the park's uthern boundary.

Just before you reach a road, a track leads northwards through the trees, joining another track and crossing a couple of wooden bridges. Arriving at a forest road, follow the sign for Beecraigs Loch and Balvormie Play Area. Turn right at the end of the road, swinging left to a crossroads where you follow the sign for Guthrie's Path.

Turn left just before a gate and cross the minor road a few metres later to follow a narrow aggregate path which winds slowly uphill into the trees. Turn right at the top. Leave the main path at a crossroads by a tourist information sign and take the track uphill through the trees. Bear left at a fork to go through a gap in the wall, turning right along another narrow aggregate path, then muddy track to meet with the main path again.

Turn left, passing a metal gate and following the sign for the Refuge Stone. Cross the stile at the sign for Witchcraig Wood, then bear right to head uphill through the trees to arrive back at the gate down to the memorial.

Ravencraig

Distance **2.3km** Time **45 minutes**
Terrain **unsurfaced woodland tracks, some short but steep gradients**
Map **OS Explorer 349** Access **there is no public transport to Ravencraig**

Ravencraig, situated right on the southern edge of the Bathgate Hills, is a large hilly woodland which rises to a rocky summit. Between 1750 and 1805, the site was used as a deer park by landowner Lord Hopetoun, and the walls and ditches (or ha-has) that criss-cross the area are remnants of this. By 1875, the land had passed to a wealthy captain who attempted to quarry for silver. Instead, he found limestone and copper.

The walk begins at the Ravencraig car park, a substantial lay-by on a minor road just north of Bathgate. Enter the site through the gate at the eastern end of the car park. The trees around here are mos deciduous and include oak, alder and horse chestnut; the wildlife includes badgers, foxes and stoats, and birds of prey like buzzards and sparrowhawks.

Bear left to pass a small pond thick wi bulrushes. This is home to many aquati based species such as dragonflies and damselflies. Go left to follow the track along a small hillside, rising gradually t take a wide vehicle track up the hill to a clearing. The track doubles back on itsel up the hill to continue through the woods, with the trees becoming more coniferous here to include Scots pine, larch and spruce.

Fork right, following the waymarkers zigzag uphill to a clearing. Go left then bear right to arrive at the highest point Ravencraig, around 290m above sea leve and the site of a 4000-year-old Bronze A burial cairn. The cairn, around 9m wide

Toppled stones at the cairn on top of Ravencraig

ıd 1.5m high, was discovered by a ıember of staff at West Lothian Council ı the summer of 1997, during woodland ıanagement operations. It is defined by kerb of large boulders, six of which :main in situ, while others have been isplaced and appear around the cairn.

Notwithstanding that it has been isturbed and there is a deep hole at its entre, it is thought that Bronze Age urials are likely to be present nderneath. It is amazing that the ıirn lay undiscovered for so ɔng, despite being so close to ıe major prehistoric ɔmplex at Cairnpapple, nly 1.2km to the north.

Take the path ɔwnhill from the ft side of the ıirn, turning ght at the ınction to climb ack up the hill to ıe clearing again. ontinue back down the ill, retracing the route up. ear right at a fork to continue ownhill, turning left to cross a learing and taking a track that leads ff on the right at the far end. The track ɔrks left, then immediately right, and limbs to pass to the left of a rocky utcrop where the view opens in all its anoramic glory.

To the northeast, the Forth Bridges, Aberdour, the Lomond Hills and Inchkeith can be seen; to the east, Bass Rock, Berwick Law, Edinburgh Castle and Arthur's Seat; to the south, the southern half of West Lothian spreads out, including Livingston, Bathgate and Armadale with the Pentlands presiding over the southern horizon.

Continue down the hill and straight across the crosspaths to pass the ruins of an old farm steading, a reminder of the area's agricultural heritage. Carry on along the path to return to the car park.

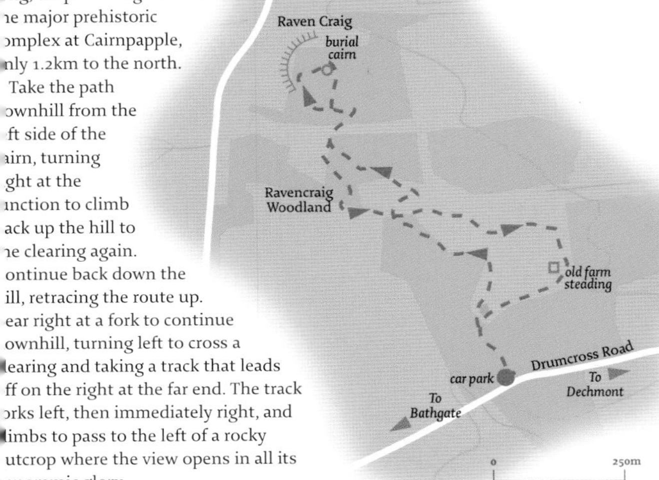

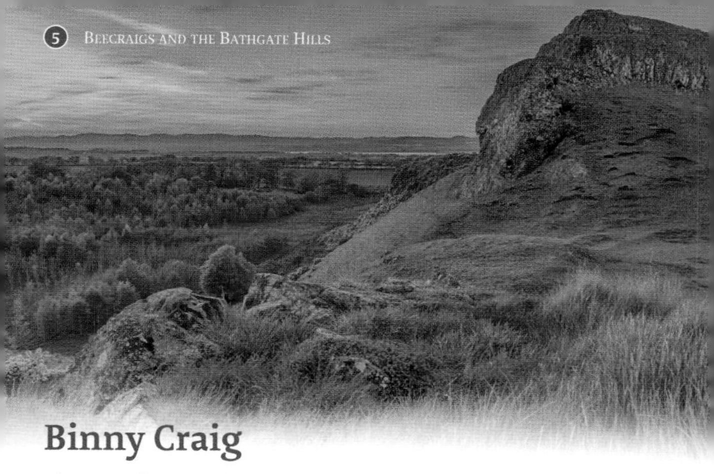

Binny Craig

Distance 4.6km Time 1 hour 15
Terrain surfaced roads, good footpaths and well-defined but occasionally muddy grassy tracks; the climb up Binny Craig itself is steep and can be slippery
Map OS Explorer 349 Access regular bus service from Linlithgow and Livingston to Ecclesmachan (disembark at the church); regular rail service to Uphall Station; the SRUC car park is only available in the evening and at weekends

During the Wars of Independence in the 13th century, Binny Craig was one in a chain of hills stretching from the Cheviots to Stirling on which burning hay bales were used as beacons to warn of the threat of invasion by English armies. This short circular route climbs to the top of the small but prominent hill.

Rising to a height of 221m, Binny Craig sits within the grounds of the Oatridge Campus of Scotland's Rural College (SRUC), near the village of Ecclesmachan. The college trains young people who want to work on the land, offering a wide range of courses, including agriculture, animal care, engineering, environment and conservation, equine studies, horticulture and landscaping.

Turn left out of the main car park of the SRUC and walk up the road, following the signs for the Scottish National Equestrian Centre. On the right, the National Path Demonstration Site, where landowners who are developing their own routes can view different types of gates and paths, is an interesting diversion.

Pass the Equestrian Centre to reach Oatridge Farm, which is used for practical tuition and includes commercially-run beef, sheep, pig and arable enterprises. Turn left to follow the road past Oatridge Golf Course, turning right onto a minor road at the end.

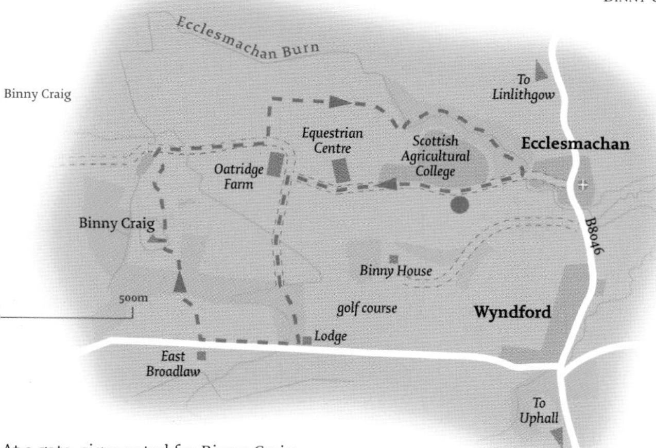

At a gate, signposted for Binny Craig,
›llow the path through a series of gates
ı a narrow track between two fields and
› a set of steps, emerging into a short
›rse-lined passage which leads to a field.
nny Craig now looms ahead.

The hill has the distinctive crag and tail
rmation of a volcanic plug that has been
orn away by the westward movement of
aciers through Scotland's Central Belt
ıring the last ice age some 12,000 years
;o. Similar formations can be seen in the
ags at Edinburgh and Stirling Castles,
ıd at Abbey Craig, by Stirling, site of the
allace Monument. All of these are
early visible from the top.

Follow the grassy track up towards
nny Craig and climb the short but steep
ll to reach the trig point at the top.
e crags are a nesting place for kestrels,
well as buzzards, sparrowhawks, merlin
d peregrine falcon, and are also home
badgers, foxes, brown hares, stoats and
weasels. If you are lucky, you may even
see a red squirrel. Most obvious of all
are the ubiquitous sheep, part of the flock
belonging to the SRUC.

Coming back down from the hill, bear left to accompany a stone wall between two gorse-covered crags and go through a gap, turning immediately right to take a muddy track through the gorse. Cross a stile, turn right and follow the farm track down the hill to turn left at a farmhouse.

Carry on down the hill to reach a signpost marked for Ecclesmachan. Cross the field here, keeping the wall to the left, passing between two fences to arrive at a more formal path, again signposted for Ecclesmachan.

At the next signpost, continue straight ahead to cross a wooden footbridge and go through the trees to return to the village and the college car park.

The Strathbrock circular

Distance 6.6km Time 1 hour 45 Terrain surfaced paths and unsurfaced tracks Map OS Explorer 349 Access bus service to Uphall from Livingston and Linlithgow; trains to Uphall Station from Edinburgh and Glasgow

The village of Broxburn originated in around 1350 when the eastern half of the Barony of Strathbrock (meaning 'the Valley of the Badgers') passed from Sir Reginald le Cheyne III to his daughter Margery. The hamlet of Eastertoun grew up around her residence and was renamed Broxburn in 1600 by Sir Richard Cockburn of Clerkington, Keeper of the Privy Seal of Scotland. This woodland walk explores the hills above Strathbrock.

The walk begins in the village of Uphall, known historically as Wester Strathbrock but now part of a conurbation with the neighbouring village of Broxburn, whicl was known as Easter Strathbrock. Both were rural communities until the 19th century when they grew rapidly followi the discovery of shale oil in the area. When the oil industry declined in the 1920s, both villages suffered in the depression that followed, but their fortunes picked up again after World Wa Two, with increased local industry and t fast growth of Livingston.

Starting at the community centre on Strathbrock Place (signposted from Uphall's West Main Street), turn left ont St Andrews Drive and follow it to the corner, where a grassy path leads right beside a fence. Follow the sign for Upha Community Woodland and, further on, turn right at a T-junction. Some of the woodland here is more than 60 years ol but most of it is young trees and incluc lots of hawthorn and broom.

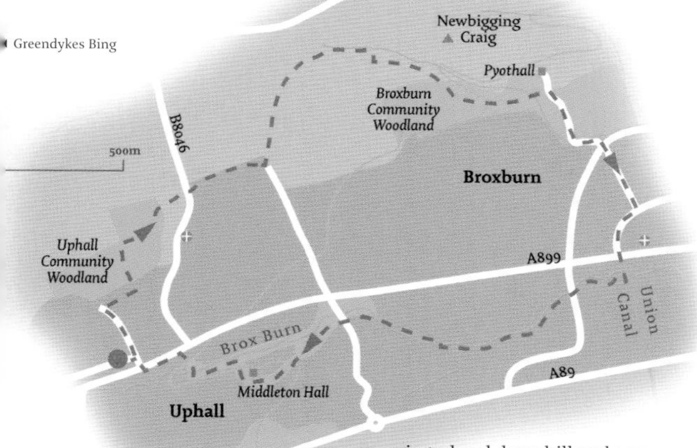

Cross Ecclesmachan Road and skirt
long the grass, turning left at the sign for
'roxburn Community Woodland.

As in Uphall, this contains mostly
oung broadleaf trees such as oak, ash,
ilver birch, alder and rowan along with
ome Scots pine. There are deer in the
voods, which feed on the plentiful supply
f brambles while sparrowhawks prey on
maller birds such as finches, tits and
parrows. In the summer, bumblebees
nd small tortoiseshell butterflies alight
n the wildflowers.

Bear left at a fork to arrive at a clearing
vith great views to Greendykes Bing and
cross Broxburn to the distant Pentlands.
ork left again to pass rowan trees and
aspberry and gorse bushes.The path goes
ownhill towards a wire fence before
winging to the right to arrive at a fork;
eep right here to go uphill again.

At the crosspaths, go left and then left again to head downhill and across a footbridge. After another climb, go through a gate and follow the track downhill. Arriving in Broxburn, walk down Pyothall Road to shortly follow the canal underneath Bridge 26, and turn right at a sign to walk along the Brox Burn Path.

Bear right to cross the burn at Holmes Court, still following the Brox Burn Path, before crossing a metal footbridge into woodland. Cross two roads to head downhill past Middleton Hall Care Home.

Middleton Hall was built in 1710 for the Reverend George Barclay who lived there after his retirement. It passed to the Earl of Buchan in 1714 and was sold to the Broxburn Oil Company in 1898, who let it out as a lunatic asylum.

Pick up the Brox Burn Path again at the bottom of the hill, continuing through woodland before crossing a bridge and arriving back at Uphall West Main Street. Walk west, turning up St Andrews Drive to return to the start.

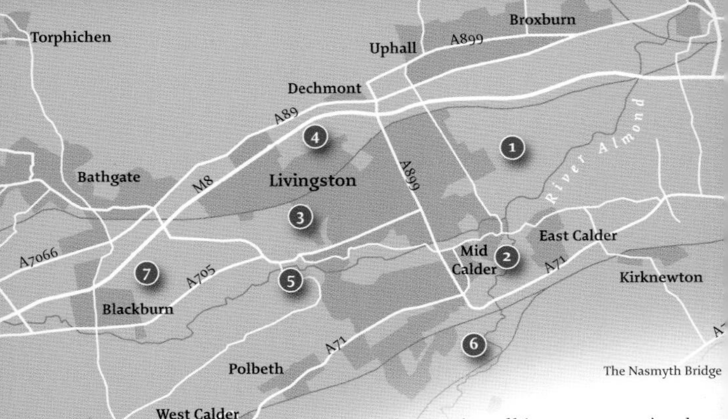

The Nasmyth Bridge

At the end of World War Two, Livingston was a small village on the River Almond. It had a church, an old mill and an inn, all dating from the 17th century. All three still stand, with the mill, now known as the Almond Valley Heritage Centre, home to the excellent Museum of the Scottish Shale Oil Industry.

The inn is a reminder that the main turnpike road through West Lothian passed through Livingston before crossing the Almond at Mid Calder and heading through East Calder and Wilkieston and on into Edinburgh.

After passing through East Calder, the turnpike passed the entrance to Almondell, an estate built by the Lord Advocate Henry Erskine along the valley of the River Almond so that he could relax at his home in the country, away from the pressures of work. Today, Erskine's mansion has gone, but visitors to Almondell Country Park, the current incarnation of his estate, can enjoy the same peace and relaxation in the grounds that he designed, as well as in the adjoining Calderwood, once the estate of the Lords of Torphichen.

Shale mining was not nearly as common here as it was a little to the north, as Livingston sits at the southern edge of the great oil shale field that underlies much of West Lothian. But the industry was still present, with oil works growing up at Oakbank and at Pumpherston. A railway was built to serve the Pumpherston Oil Works and the lime works at Camps by East Calder, slicing across Erskine's Almondell Estate in a high and impressive viaduct, the route of which provides further walking opportunities.

In 1962 Livingston was chosen as the site of Scotland's fourth New Town and grew rapidly, swallowing neighbouring villages, and in the 1970s and '80s it was at the heart of the 'Silicon Glen' technology boom when many foreign electronics companies chose Scotland as their base.

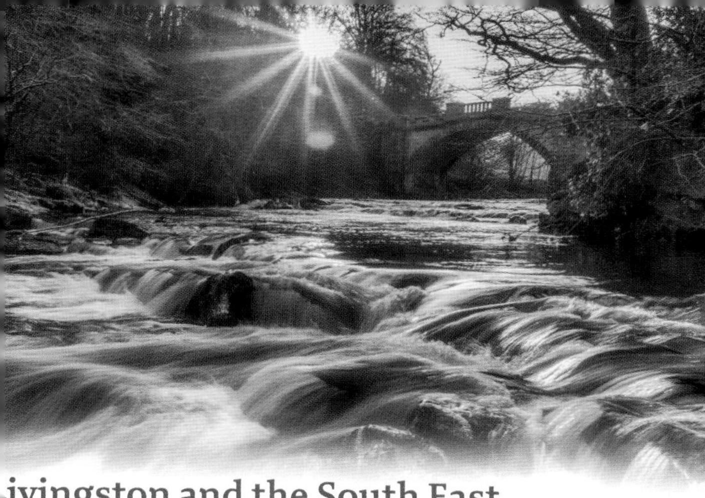

ivingston and the South East

The Camps Branch Railway

Distance 9.2km Time 2 hours 30 Terrain good footpaths, some muddy, some minor roads Maps OS Explorer 349 and 350 Access regular bus service to East Calder from Livingston and Edinburgh

Follow the route of the old North British Railway line over Camps Viaduct to Uphall, returning through the beautiful Almondell Country Park.

There have been limestone quarries at Raw Camps, around 1.5km east of East Calder, since at least 1760. By the 1860s, it was home to the largest limestone quarry in Scotland. Lime was transported from the site to the Union Canal at Lin's Mill Aqueduct, where it was taken on to Edinburgh. With the coming of the railways, the North British Railway built a 3.6km branch line from Uphall Station, linking Camps to Pumpherston Oil Works and the main Edinburgh to Bathgate Line. It opened in June 1867.

The walk follows the route of the line, starting at the Almondell & Calderwood Country Park south car park. Return to the main road and follow it back toward East Calder to join the railway at Almondell Grove.

Follow the path over the Camps Viadu with fantastic views up and down the river. Built in 1885, the viaduct's nine spans carried the line some 23m above t River Almond. The canal feeder splits from the river on the left, and on the rig the iron aqueduct that carries the feeder across the river is obvious.

Although Raw Camps Quarry ceased production in 1937, the Camps Branch Line remained open until January 1959 when the line beyond Pumpherston was closed, rendering the Camps Viaduct redundant. The category B-listed structu has since become home to colonies of bats and badgers.

Further on, two sets of brick pillars are the remains of roadbridges for the Pumpherston Oil Works. In 1882 a refine

'he Camps Viaduct,
Almondell

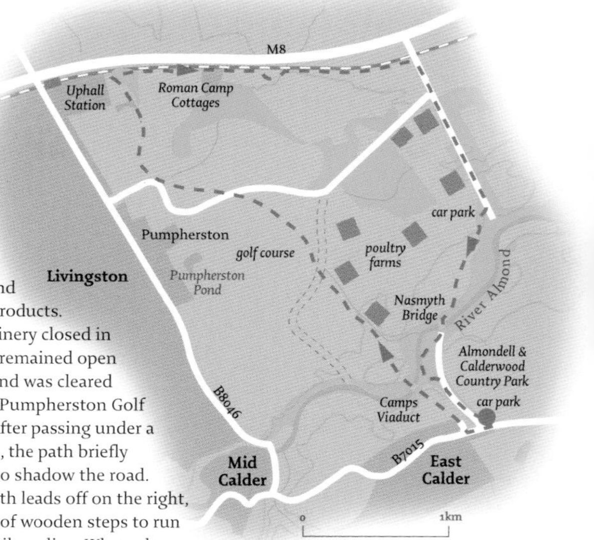

ıs established
Pumpherston,
tracting crude
from shale
erations
over West
thian to refine
:o road fuels and
her oil-based products.
though the refinery closed in
64, the railway remained open
til 1981. The land was cleared
d reopened as Pumpherston Golf
urse in 2002. After passing under a
one roadbridge, the path briefly
ns westwards to shadow the road.
Eventually a path leads off on the right,
scending a set of wooden steps to run
st beside the railway line. Where the
th joins a minor road, continue straight
ead to reach the rows of cottages of
man Camp. Despite the name, there is
evidence that there was ever a Roman
mp here. The cottages were built in
90 by the Broxburn Oil Company to
use the staff of their new Roman Camp
Works, which opened in 1889. The
rks closed in 1956.
oining a main road, cross over and turn
ht towards Almondell & Calderwood
untry Park, passing the Wallace Stone
t beyond a lay-by on the right which
arks where William Wallace observed
English troops gathering before the
ttle of Falkirk in 1298. Turn into the car
k and go through the exit by the
noticeboard. Keep right, continuing through the woods along the edge of Almondell.

Descending to a surfaced path, turn right to cross the Dell Bridge and continue, swinging over the Nasmyth Bridge. Also known as the Almondell Bridge, it was commissioned in around 1802 by the lawyer and MP Henry Erskine, who owned the estate of Almondell, and designed by his friend, the artist Alexander Nasmyth.

Take the path for Mid Calder, Livingston and Bathgate, bearing left at a fork to reach the canal feeder aqueduct. Climb the steps and follow the path through the woodland to the left, turning uphill on reaching the main path back to the car park.

The Calderwood Birch Trail

Distance 4.9km Time 1 hour 15 Terrain mostly forest tracks, some very muddy underfoot Map OS Explorer 349 Access regular bus service to Mid Calder from Livingston and Edinburgh

Undeveloped and unspoilt, Calderwood sits on a plateau bounded by the steep, wooded valleys of the Linhouse and Murieston Waters. Trees such as oak, hazel, ash, rowan, wild cherry, hawthorn, beech and birch cover much of the plateau and the rich mixture of woodland, wetland and grassland provides a home for roe deer, fox, heron, woodpecker, bats and badgers. Explore the largest area of ancient woodland in West Lothian, and one of its best kept secrets, on this walk.

There has been woodland in Calderwood for many hundreds of years. In the 1500s, trees were coppiced for charcoal and oak was harvested for shipbuilding, in the 1700s, drovers reste[d] their cattle here before taking them ove[r] the Pentland Hills, and in the 1900s, the area was mined for shale oil.

Throughout this time, the site belong[ed] to the powerful Sandilands family who owned the lands of Calder and who, as t[he] Lords Torphichen, live in Calder House i[n] Mid Calder to this day. West Lothian Council took over management in the la[te] 1960s and it was designated a Site of Special Scientific Interest by Scottish Natural Heritage in 1988.

The walk starts in Almondell & Calderwood Country Park's Mid Calder c[ar] park and follows the green waymarkers around the park. Head towards Almond[ell] from the car park, leaving the path at th[e] sign for Calderwood and Oakbank to follow a muddy path along the east ban[k] of the Linhouse Water. Bear right to go beneath one of the two arches of the Ea[st] Bridge, built in 1794 to replace a ford in

ılderwood

ː river between East and Mid Calder. ːross the footbridge back over the ıhouse Water, then another footbridge, s time over the Murieston Water, which ws into the Linhouse Water just a few ːtres from this point. From here a track ds uphill. Bear left at an information ard, passing a large pond on the right. ›gs, toads and newts return to the nd in spring to breed, and the vae of invertebrates like ıgonflies live under the water. an optional detour, follow ː track on the left opposite the nd to reach an attractive little terfall at a bend on the ıhouse Water.
ʼhe path curves gradually ht, crossing a vast clearing d wandering back into the trees, still lowing the green waymarkers. Bear ː at the fork, sticking to the ymarked path and ignoring the riad of minor paths that leave the ıin trail. Head along the top of the rge of the Murieston Water, lowing a tree-lined avenue to ɔther information board. ddenly the track emerges into ː daylight, with some ʼgantuan ancient beech es straight ahead. ntinue past a copse of ver birch to arrive at a ge grassland which ›vides shelter for small mammals and is a hunting ground for birds of prey such as buzzards, kestrels and sparrowhawks.

Continue straight ahead past a small tree-covered hill to descend steeply back to join the outward route at the first information board. Turn left to retrace your steps to the car park.

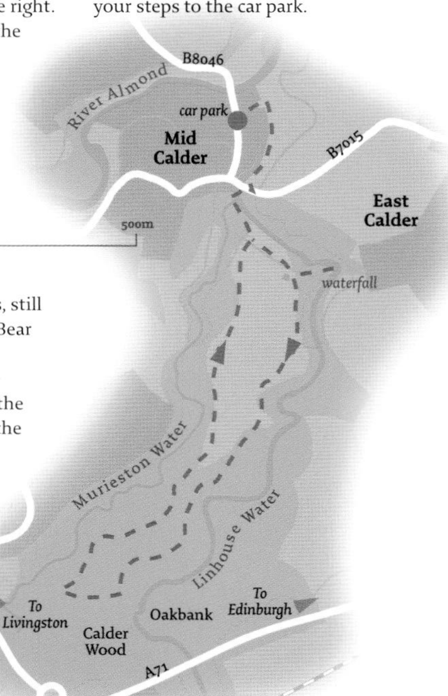

Eliburn Reservoir and the River Almon

Distance **6.1km** Time **1 hour 45**
Terrain **mostly good surfaced paths and unsurfaced tracks, some muddy**
Map **OS Explorer 349** Access **regular bus and rail services to Livingston from Edinburgh and Glasgow**

The original village of Livingston sat on the banks of the River Almond and its 18th-century inn, where Robert Burns found the inspiration for his song 'The Bonnie Lass of Livingston', is a reminder that it was on the stagecoach route from Edinburgh to Glasgow. In 1962, the village gave its name to the New Town that was to grow up around it. This is an unexpectedly rural walk, passing along the wooded banks of both a small reservoir and the River Almond.

From the front of the Livingston FC Community Club at Eliburn Park, follow the path past the car park and into the woodland to walk around Eliburn Reservoir. This picturesque reservoir is awash with waterlilies and home to ma waterbirds. The woodland has been her since at least 1860.

Reaching the end of the reservoir, go straight over the crosspaths to zigzag downhill, turning left to follow the Lochshot Burn Path and, later, beari right to pass beneath three bridges. Tur left at the end of the path, descending t the right just before a barrier across the road. Bear left to walk along the banks c the River Almond.

Cross a road and keep right to contin along the riverbank for 300m, emerging into a large park. Cross a footbridge ove the Folly Burn and swing gently uphill, climbing the steps to cross Livingston Village Main Street. Continue up the pa and go through an underpass, turning right and then left at the junction, following the sign for Alderstone Path.

Cross a small steel-railed bridge to th left, continuing straight ahead to go through another underpass, turning rig

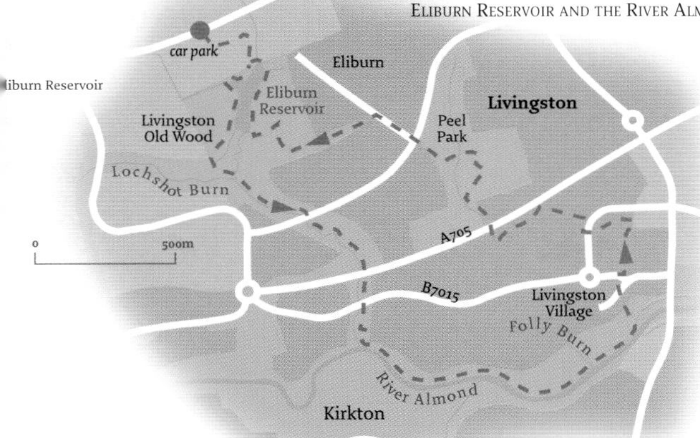

en left to follow the path uphill to nerge onto Kirkfield View. Bear right, llowing the sign for the Follyburn Path, hich spirals round onto a footbridge. Fork left, then turn right at the osspaths, passing around the undations on the left. These ruins mark e site of Livingston House, but were uilt in the early 1990s. The house itself ated from 1671 and was demolished in ound 1840. Its surroundings were ndscaped with oak trees and conifers, any of them still standing.

Climb the mound, which marks the site Livingston Peel, a square stone werhouse, or peel (from the French *piel* r a 'fortified fence' or 'palisade'), built in ound 1124 by a Flemish nobleman amed De Leving, who was granted the nd by King David I. The servants' ttages that grew up around the tower ecame known as Leving's Toun, from hich Livingston got its name.

The peel's final occupant was Sir Patrick Murray, a horticulturist and collector of rare flowers, shrubs and trees. Following his death, his friends Sir Andrew Balfour and Sir Robert Sibbald transplanted his garden to Edinburgh, where it became known as the Physic Garden, due to Sibbald's interest in herbal medicines. Today, it is known as Edinburgh's Royal Botanic Garden.

Come down from the mound and bear left, going straight over a crosspaths to cross a bridge and head uphill and through an underpass. Cross two roads and walk along the end of a cul-de-sac, turning left to pass briefly through woodland before crossing another road and continuing straight ahead. Return to a surfaced path for a few metres before continuing straight ahead at the crosspaths.

Turn right at a junction, taking the track straight ahead at the next to dive through the thicket, bearing right. Turn left to drop to the reservoir and walk up the east bank, retracing your steps to the start.

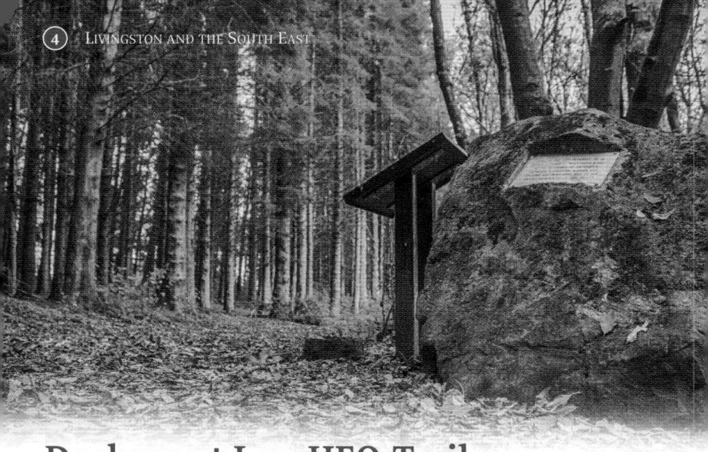

Dechmont Law UFO Trail

Distance 2.4km Time 45 minutes Terrain surfaced paths, unsurfaced woodland tracks, one optional steep climb Map OS Explorer 349 Access regular bus and rail services to Livingston from Edinburgh and Glasgow

The Dechmont Woods Encounter is unique in British legal history as the only example of an 'alien encounter' becoming the subject of a criminal investigation. This walk takes you to the site of the incident, a hallowed spot for Britain's many ufologists.

Around 10:30am on 9 November 1979, forestry worker Bob Taylor was walking his red setter along the path beside Dechmont Law when he saw a large sphere of around 6.4m wide hovering above the forest floor. Two smaller spheres of around 90cm wide emerged and pulled him by the legs towards the large sphere, causing him to lose consciousness. When he woke 20 minut later, the sphere had gone and his dog was barking furiously. Returning to his truck, he could not get it to start, so he walked to his home in Livingston.

On seeing his dishevelled appearance and the rips in his heavy work trousers, his wife contacted the police, who returned to the site of the incident with him. There were marks in the ground where he said the various spheres had been. The tears in his clothing were consistent with having been dragged by the ankles. The police were completely baffled and the case, which remains ope was recorded as criminal assault.

Bob Taylor, who was well-respected in his local community, never changed his story or belief in what happened right u to his death in 2007, aged 88.

To find the site of the encounter start

plaque marks the site of the 'encounter'

m the car park just beyond Deans mmunity High School in Livingston. through the wooden gate and follow path uphill. Bear right at the fork, lowing the path through a gateway into North Woods, a varied woodland of amore, beech and oak. In the spring, forest floor is carpeted with bluebells. ollow the track through the woods to ch a stone pyramid, turning left, then aring right to follow the path downhill a crosspaths. An information point d a memorial stone mark the location the incident.

'urn right to return to the stone ramid and follow the path back to gateway. Continue along a track through the grass towards chmont Law.

Cross a small embankment before hort but steep climb to the top the hill. Like Binny Craig, chmont Law is a volcanic plug d bears the same distinctive crag d tail formation. There are traces of onze and Iron Age agricultural terracing its slopes and a few small signs ggesting that a hillfort might once have od on its summit. Although its ategic position makes this likely, any nclusive archaeological evidence has en lost through years of quarrying. spite its modest height, the 360-degree w from the top of 'Decky Hill', as it is own locally, is well worth the minimal ort required.

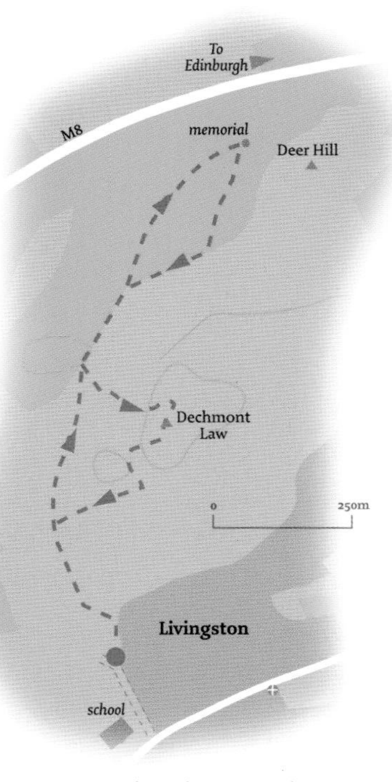

Turn right from the viewing disc, following the steep path back down the hill. Some rough steps have been dug into the earth to make the descent easier. Cross the embankment and return to the main path and back to the car park. Hopefully you won't encounter any extraterrestrial spaceships on the way.

The Killandean and Almond circuit

Distance 8.6km Time 2 hours 15
Terrain good surfaced footpaths, unsurfaced footpaths, farm track
Map OS Explorer 344 Access bus to the Killandean Community Allotments from Livingston town centre

Livingston was the fourth New Town created in Scotland to deal with the overspill from Glasgow's densely populated city centre in the years following the Second World War. Today it has a population greater than that of Perth, Stirling or Inverness. This enjoyable riverside ramble explores the quiet countryside west of the town.

The West Calder Burn rises on Pates Hill and merges with Limefield Water at Gavieside, where it becomes known as the Killandean Burn. It flows into Livingston from Gavieside, giving its name to the Killandean Community Allotments.

This route begins at the allotments car park, which is down a short slip road where Simpson Parkway (B7015) crosses the Killandean Burn. From the car park, take the path beneath the bridge, then climb to cross it and go back under agai on the far side. Continue eastwards, turning left onto the road to cross two bridges in quick succession, over the Killandean Burn and the River Almond. The two merge a few metres downstrea

Rising at Easter Hassockrigg, on Benh Moor north of Shotts, the River Almond runs eastwards through Polkemmet Country Park before passing through Whitburn and Blackburn and onwards t Livingston. Beyond here it runs throug the deep valley of Almondell before passing below the Lin's Mill Aqueduct a Almond Valley Viaduct at Newbridge an the Almond Viaduct at Kirkliston, finall flowing into the Forth at Cramond.

Turn left along the riverbank, keeping left to later cross a wooden bridge and further on head beneath a large metal bridge that crosses the river. The histori buildings of the Almond Valley Heritag Centre are on the right. This was

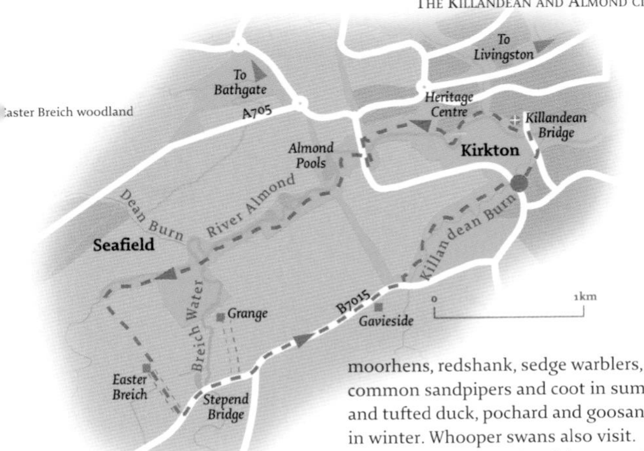

:aster Breich woodland

'iginally a mill which began production around 1770 but was derelict by the 60s when a team of local enthusiasts set out its restoration. A city farm was oon established and the Scottish Shale l Museum, celebrating West Lothian's nale oil industry, was housed in one of e outbuildings. The mill, farm and oil useum were combined in 1990 to form e Almond Valley Heritage Centre.

Follow the farm road through the eld beside the narrow-gauge track the heritage centre's preserved railway. slender path continues straight ahead wards Almondhaugh Halt – the end of e line for the railway. The path leads off ft to continue along the riverbank efore climbing to cross a roadbridge. urn left through the trees to go back own the hill and under the bridge. Bear ght, then left at the forks.

Passing the Almond Pools, look out for moorhens, redshank, sedge warblers, common sandpipers and coot in summer and tufted duck, pochard and goosander in winter. Whooper swans also visit.

Continue straight ahead for around 1.5km, passing a sign for Easter Breich Woodland. The path here is lined with rowan, oak and beech trees. Look out for chiffchaff, willow warblers, whitethroats and garden warblers, as well as deer, wood mice and squirrels.

Keep right at the fork, then left to cross a wooden footbridge, continuing towards Seafield and Blackburn. Take the path towards Westwood (the Five Sisters Bing), following a farm track to Easter Breich and on to the main B7015 road. Cross and turn left, joining a footpath after around 100m, just beyond the cottages. At the junction, turn left towards Livingston. At the traffic lights beyond Gavieside Farm, cross the road and take the Killandean Path.

The path leads through the trees and along a concrete walkway on the banks of the Killandean Burn. Bear right to pass the allotments before going under the bridge and back to the car park.

The Linn Jaw loop

Distance 11.3km **Time** 3 hours
Terrain mostly unsurfaced tracks, with some minor roads **Map** OS Explorer 344
Access no public transport to the start, but it is possible to walk from Mid Calder via the Calderwood Birch Trail

Climb a shale bing before exploring the Linhouse Glen Nature Reserve and visiting the Linn Jaw Falls, one of the area's best kept secrets.

Beginning at Calderwood Country Park's Oakbank car park, take the path past the information board, bearing right to reach the top of the bing with splendid views towards Greendykes Bing, the Forth Bridges and Fife.

Oakbank Oil Works, strategically situated beside the Caledonian Railway's Edinburgh to Glasgow Line, was established in 1864. Shale was obtained from small-scale shale workings in Calderwood, then from two pits north of the works which were connected by a private railway. An aerial ropeway also linked the works to pits at Newfarm to th west. Demolished in around 1932, all that remains of the works is the bing.

Head along the brow of the hill and down a set of steps constructed out of ol railway sleepers, turning left at the bottom to pass below the A71. Continue up the path to pass below one arch of a railway viaduct. Bear left at the fork to follow the path for 1km, turning left towards Linhouse Glen Nature Reserve at the sign and walking along the embankment beside the muddy vehicle track. Carefully cross the railway at the level crossing and follow the wide track down until almost at the edge of the woodland, turning right just before you exit the trees to walk along a corridor of mature beech trees.

Linn Jaw Waterfall

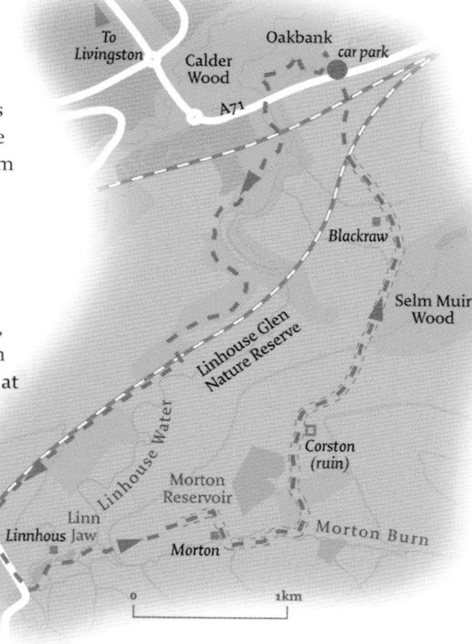

The track soon narrows to pass
long the side of the fence by the
ilway line but widens after 100m
lead through woodland.
eaching a fence, walk back
wards the railway where a gap
lows you to pass through.
Follow a wide but muddy
ack along the side of moorland,
riving eventually at a gate. Turn
ft to follow the road, going left at
small lay-by to take the
otpath along the north bank
the Camilty Water.
Through the trees to the
ft is Linnhous. This
autiful manor house
as built as an L-plan
werhouse in 1589 by
ancis Tennent of Mukraw,
former Provost of Edinburgh.
1631, the property had passed to the
uirhead family. In the 17th century, a
cond L-plan towerhouse was joined
the original to create a substantial
plan mansion.
After about 400m, cross a footbridge
d continue eastwards, bearing right to
through a gate and cross the burn.
llow the fence, going through a gate in
e top corner and returning to the river.
The path climbs along the edge of a
rge with some spectacular waterfalls
low. You can, optionally, scramble
wn to the riverbank where a fence
sses the path to see the Linn Jaw Falls.
The walls of the narrow gorge tower majestically overhead, with trees at the top on all three sides.

Climb out of the gorge and over the low fence, crossing the field and turning left at the gate to follow the track between two fences.

Turn left, following the road round past another gate, passing the ruined remains of Corston Farm on the hillside. Selm Muir Wood is on the right. Cross a railway bridge before descending to cross the A71. Take the path towards Oakbank Village.

At a sign for Oakbank, turn left and follow a narrow path uphill to return to the car park.

Seafield Law and Easter Inch Moss

Distance 6.1km Time 1 hour 45
Terrain surfaced footpaths and well-defined tracks Map OS Explorer 349
Access regular bus service to Seafield from Livingston

Scotland contains around 18 percent of the world's peatlands; they are Scotland's rainforest. Seafield Law and Easter Inch Moss became West Lothian's first Local Nature Reserve in 2007 and work is underway at the moss to raise water levels by constructing dams and removing birch scrub to restore this important Lowland peat bog.

The walk begins at the Seafield Law car park, accessed off the A705 at Seafield, between Whitburn and Livingston. Return to the main road and turn left, walking through the village and going left at a battered old sign for Seafield Law.

This was the site of Seafield Patent Oil Works, which operated between 1874 and 1951 and was served by a railway line which branched south from the Edinburgh to Bathgate Line across Easter Inch Moss towards Blackburn. A further line branched off east towards the oil works. The route of these lines is now a surfaced public path along the south side of the former Seafield Bing and Easter Inch Moss, and across the moss itself towards Bathgate.

Seafield Bing was the pile of spent shale from the oil works. Lowered and reshaped in 1996 so it would blend into the landscape with a crag and tail much like Binny Craig or Dechmont Law, it was renamed Seafield Law. The 'crag' still shows the red shale of the bing, but the rest of the hill has been planted with grasses, flowers, shrubs and trees.

Cross the path and follow the footpath towards the hill. Approaching the summit, turn right to reach the top.

After enjoying the view, turn around and follow the track straight back down the hill to return to the path, turning right along the line of the former railway and ignoring the path that comes in from th

Easter Inch Moss

eft. Bear left at the next junction and ontinue along the path, taking a sharp ight just before reaching some houses o walk up a dirt track across the moor, earing right again to cut diagonally cross the moorland.

The Mosside Peat and Litter Company tarted peat extraction at Easter Inch Moss in 1916. The railway that served the il works also served the peat extraction ompany until the operation was closed n 1956. There was over a mile of narrow-auge railway track across the moss, onveying peat from the point of xtraction to the preparation centre where was bagged and sold on for orticultural and other purposes.

This operation left the moss a shadow f its former glory. A healthy peat bog bsorbs and stores carbon from the tmosphere and contributes greatly in the battle against global warming. However, an unhealthy, dry peat bog releases the carbon. Scotland's peat bogs are estimated to hold more than 3000 million tons of carbon, but around 10 million tonnes are being released back into the atmosphere each year.

More than 140 different species of plant can be found at Easter Inch, including 11 that are rare in West Lothian. Many species of bird also live here, including reed buntings, skylarks and short-eared owls. The moss is also home to butterflies, moths and damselflies, roe deer, brown hare, water vole and otters, and frogs, toads and newts.

Turn left at a crosspaths. Where an embankment comes in from the left, take the path to the right to meet with a surfaced path. Turn right, then bear left to return to the car park.

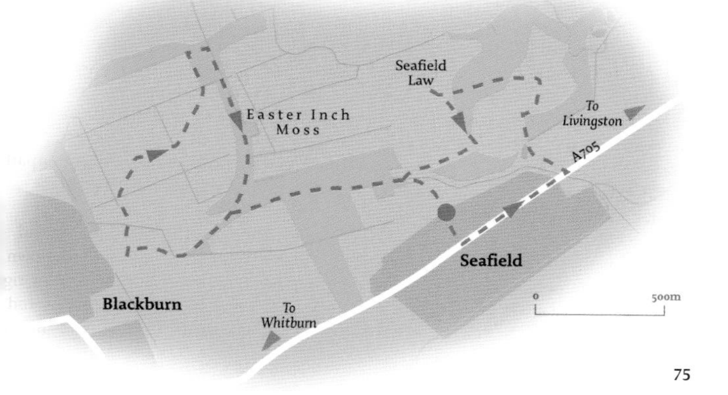

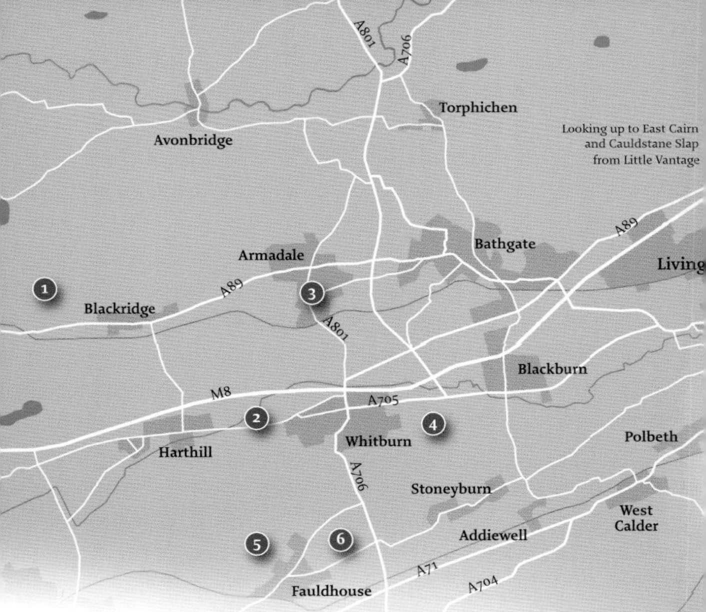

Looking up to East Cairn
and Cauldstane Slap
from Little Vantage

The land south of Armadale is mostly moorland, stretching all the way into the Pentlands. While much of it has been taken over by commercial forestry plantations, a great deal of apparently unspoilt moor remains.

But just as in the rest of West Lothian, signs of industry abound. The land was home to coalmining, but ironstone was also mined here, supplying the ironworks across the border in Lanarkshire. Whinstone was quarried here too and transported to Edinburgh for building works. The route of the railway that served these long-gone industries is the basis for two of the walks in this chapter.

The hills of the western Pentlands are much quieter and more desolate than their brethren at the eastern end of the range. While the eastern Pentlands are also volcanic in origin, the bedrock beneath the moor-clad slopes to the west of East Cairn and the Cauldstane Slap is composed of Devonian Old Red Sandstone.

Despite being so close to civilisation – Livingston is only a few kilometres away – it is possible to walk for hours on these hills without meeting another soul. It was not always this way. Two of the walks in this chapter follow traditional routes across the Pentlands, used for centuries to head south to the Borders and on into England.

'he South West and the Pentlands

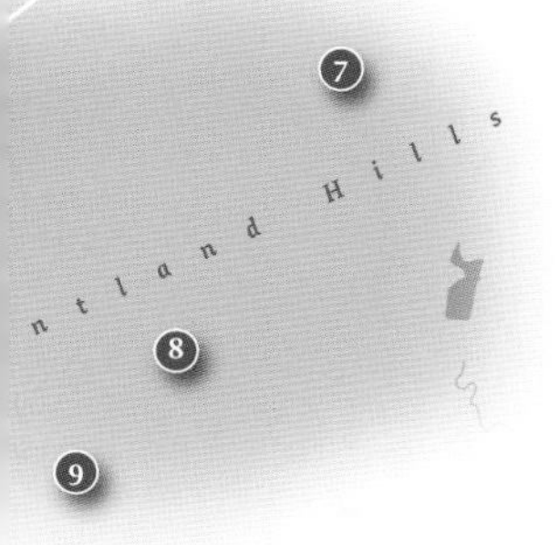

Blawhorn Moss

Distance 4.3km Time 1 hour 15 Terrain good surfaced paths and unsurfaced tracks Map OS Explorer 349 Access regular bus and rail services to Blackridge from Bathgate

The hidden gem that is Blawhorn Moss National Nature Reserve, high on the hills behind Blackridge, is one of the best examples of a Lowland raised bog in Central Scotland. These bogs once covered vast swathes of the Scottish Lowlands, but few remain. It is so quiet and peaceful here that it is easy to forget that you are right in the middle of the busiest part of Scotland.

Bogs begin as shallow muddy lochs in hollows gouged out by glaciers. Plants such as reeds and mosses grow and die, but the waterlogged ground stops them from rotting. More plants grow and die, creating layer upon layer of dead plant material and forming peat. As a bog accumulates peat, it acts as a carbon sink contributing to the fight against climate change. While other peat bogs have been exploited over the centuries, Blawhorn Moss has remained relatively untouched and it is now being actively managed. Sheep graze the surface to stop the spread of scrub and trees and encourage sphagnum mosses. Ditches are dammed and artificial barriers help raise the water table to encourage the bog to grow.

From the Blawhorn Moss car park off the A89, just west of Blackridge, go through the gate and follow a long track lined with beech trees. At a junction, ignore the sign marked 'Footpath' and continue up the hill.

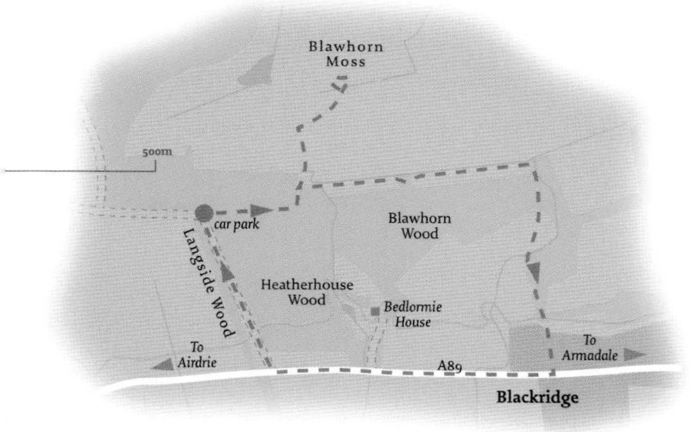

Go through the gate on the right and llow the track over a wooden bridge ross the bog. Turn right at the far end to llow a circular wooden walkway around e heather-covered, peaty moorland.

There are three steel sculptures by n Whitson around the walkway. mmissioned by Scottish Natural eritage, two of them are inspired by icroscopic views of parts of sphagnum oss. The first, named *Sporagnium*, presents the spore capsules of hair moss. The walkway widens out, crossing a ol where there is a sculpture of a agonfly. The third sculpture, named *chegonium*, represents the moss's icroscopic egg capsules.

Follow the path back around to the idge and retrace your steps to the otpath sign. Turn left to follow the path neath some beech trees and cross a tle wooden bridge beside a cattle grid. e track continues along the southern edge of Blawhorn Moss, passing through a small pocket of Scots pines. Bear right to head downhill across open grassland and another little wooden bridge over a burn.

Go through the gate and on through more woodland of Scots pine, oak, hawthorn and elm. Pass the ruins of an old farmhouse before going through a large wooden gate and following a road downhill into Blackridge. Turn right at the main road to walk along the footpath out of the village.

This was the old road between Edinburgh and Glasgow, and Blawhorn got its name from the horn that the coach between the two cities would blow to announce its arrival at the coaching inn in Blackridge.

Carry on along the path to reach a sign for Blawhorn Moss Nature Reserve. Turn right to follow the single-track road uphill back to the car park.

im Whitson's *Dragonfly* and *Sporagnium* sculptures

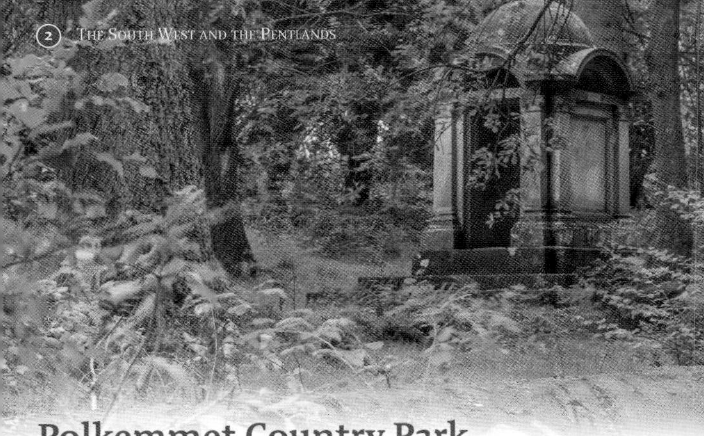

Polkemmet Country Park

Distance **4.1km** Time **1 hour 15**
Terrain **good surfaced paths and unsurfaced tracks** Map **OS Explorer 343**
Access **regular bus service from Livingston to the park entrance**

This walk explores the beautiful Polkemmet Country Park, which sits in the former Polkemmet Estate, home of the Baillie family for many years.

The Polkemmet Estate began in 1620 when the Baillie family purchased the land. By the 19th century, the estate was thriving and the 1871 census shows that Polkemmet House had 39 rooms, with 11 servants. During World War Two, the estate became an army camp and then afterwards a residential school, before being taken over by the Scottish Police College. The estate was sold to the National Coal Board in 1960 with a view to exploiting the coal seams that lie beneath it. Polkemmet House was demolished and the estate grew derelict until it was acquired by the regional council in 1978.

After restoring the site to its former glory, Polkemmet Country Park opened to the public in June 1981 with the buildings that had formerly been offices and stables converted into a visitor centre. This is home to the Scottish Owl Centre, where you will find the world's largest collection of owls.

The steam engine on display in front o the visitor centre was built in 1909 by Andrew Barclay of Kilmarnock and name *Dardanelles* after the World War I campaig in progress when Polkemmet Colliery opened. It spent most of its working life at the colliery before being put on displa at Polkemmet Country Park as a war memorial in 1981.

Leaving the visitor centre turn right towards the driving range. The road quickly becomes a path as it enters woodland. The path swings left to the

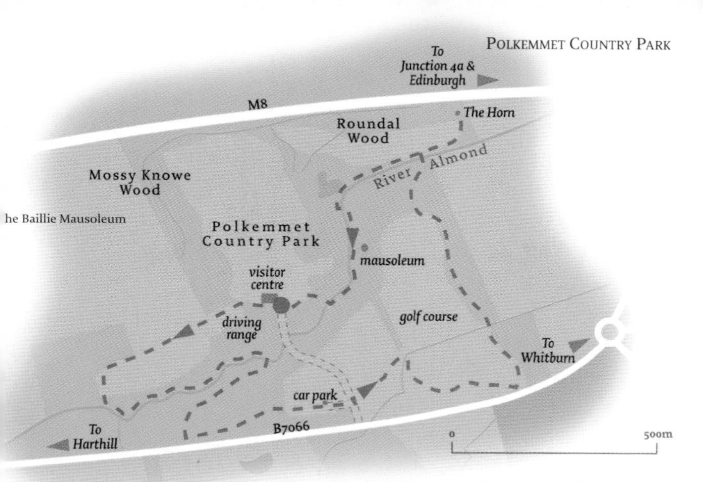

ver Almond which runs through the
tire length of Polkemmet Country Park
d is home to wildlife such as heron,
ngfishers and otters.

Bear right at a fork to stay by the
erbank, crossing it by a bridge and
ading for the Dumback Entrance. Bear
t and go across the car park, before
ossing the road to follow the path
ound the golf course. Keep right to cross
bridge and go around the southern and
stern edges of the course. Turn right at
rosspaths to head down through the
es, before crossing a footbridge, and
ing through a gateway. Walk around the
ge of the field to reach The Horn.

This 24m-high tubular stainless-steel
ucture overlooks the westbound
riageway of the M8 motorway.
signed by Scottish artists Matthew
lziel and Louise Scullion, it was
stalled in 1997 as part of the M8 Art
Project. Return to the gateway, turning right to pass a pond before going left to cross the river again.

Passing through a copse of Western red cedar, the Baillie Mausoleum appears on the left. This mausoleum was erected in 1915 by Lady Baillie of Polkemmet for her husband Sir Robert Baillie, the 4th Baronet of Polkemmet, and her son Sir Gawaine Baillie, the 5th Baronet, killed in the first few days of World War One.

The family's connection with Polkemmet came to an end in 1947 with the death of Sir Adrian Baillie, the 6th Baronet, who was also interred in the family mausoleum. The remains were moved to Whitburn Churchyard in 1963 when the National Coal Board were considering mining the estate.

Continue down the path, which climbs gradually to a set of stone steps. Cross the river and follow the road uphill back to the visitor centre.

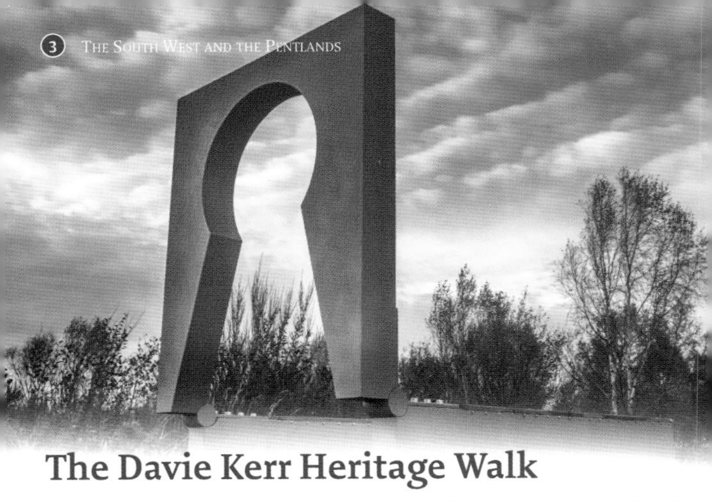

The Davie Kerr Heritage Walk

Distance **11.2km** Time **3 hours**
Terrain **good surfaced paths and unsurfaced tracks** Map **OS Explorer 349**
Access **regular bus and rail services to Armadale from Livingston**

Davie Kerr was a local historian, councillor, poet and Scots language enthusiast who devised this walk around his home town, calling it 'A Daunder Round Armadale'.

The town of Armadale was originally an estate known as Barbauchlaw but it changed name when it was bought by Sir William Honeyman, later to become Lord Armadale after his family estate in Sutherland.

From the Cross in Armadale, walk up North Street before turning onto Bridgecastle Road, then Baird Drive. Continue straight ahead along the track, bearing right and following the Armadale Round Town Path along the edge of the Barbauchlaw Glen with the pretty little Barbauchlaw Burn running through it.

Passing a garden centre, turn uphill, taking the path to the right, bearing right and still following the Round Tow Path through a gate and along the top o the Barbauchlaw Glen. Ogilface Castle once stood on a promontory on the hillside across the glen. Local tradition says that it was used by the Covenanter as a refuge and hideout. Much later, the village of Woodend sprung up on the hillside above the castle. Built in the 186 to house the workers of the Coltness Irc Company, it was demolished in the 195

Go through a gate and up to the main road, heading out of town and crossing the road after 50m to follow a farm track through a gate. This is the former site o the Buttries Pit, sunk by the Monklands Coal and Iron Company in the 1850s. Th

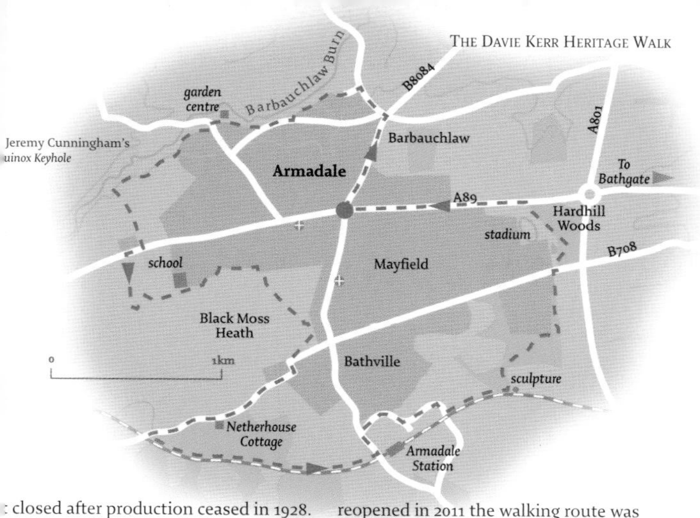

Jeremy Cunningham's
uinox Keyhole

: closed after production ceased in 1928.
Double back on yourself, bearing left to
alk alongside a fence and through a gate
emerge into a field. Turn left, passing
madale Academy on the left and the
ssocked heather-clad moorland of Black
oss on the right. Turn left again at a
aying field to go through a gap in the
dge. At the end of the road, bear right
cross Black Moss Heath, turning right
ain just beyond the entrance.

A former industrial site, native
oadleaf trees and shrubs were planted
re in the 1990s to provide a habitat for
ldlife. At the other side of the heath,
ntinue straight ahead, bearing right to
low the road out of town.

After 900m, turn left at the railway
dge, following the Airdrie to Bathgate
th. The Edinburgh and Bathgate Railway
ened in November 1849 and closed west
Bathgate in 1986. Although the line
reopened in 2011 the walking route was maintained and this path was built.

The route eventually swings sharp left to reach a roundabout, where you head down Station Way, then Southdale Avenue, returning to the railway path at the bridge. Continue along the path to reach the *Equinox Keyhole*, so called because at the equinox the shadow of the keyhole aligns with the base.

At the keyhole, turn left, bearing right at the fork to go through a gate and across a road. Rejoin the Armadale Round Town Path. This is Hardhill Woods, once the site of Hopetoun Colliery. Scouts planted the woodland in 1999 and cairns around the site identify Scotland's six scouting regions.

Bear right, continuing northwards past a pond and the Edinburgh Monarchs Speedway Stadium. Turn left to follow the road back to the Cross.

Whitrigg Bing

Distance **3.3km** Time **1 hour**
Terrain **good surfaced paths and unsurfaced tracks** Map **OS Explorer 343**
Access **regular bus services to East Whitburn from Livingston**

Whitburn was originally called Whiteburn, as opposed to Blackburn, which was situated at the eastern end of Blackburn Parish. The burn in question is the River Almond, which flows through both villages before reaching Livingston. This is an easy climb to the summit of a coal bing.

Start at the small car park on Drum Place in East Whitburn, reached from the Main Street (A705) by turning up Bathgate Road, then right onto Torbane Drive and right again onto Drum Place. Take the path downhill, turning right at the crosspaths to follow a surfaced path underneath an old railway bridge. This is part of the former line of the Wilsontown Morningside and Coltness Railway.

Just beyond the railway bridge on the right was the site of Whitburn Station, which opened in 1854 and closed in 1930.

Continue straight along the Railway Path, passing the rear of some modern housing. The surfaced path quickly becomes unsurfaced. Just beyond a staggered gateway, turn left at the signpost for Whitrigg Community Woodland Path. The path leads uphill through a beech woodland on a slope so gentle that you barely notice it. This was at one time the Whitrigg Branch Line, a short railway line which served Whitrigg Colliery.

Whitrigg Bing is the spoil from the colliery, which was also known as Lady of the Dales. It opened in around 1900, mining coal for gas production, as well as for domestic heating, manufacturing an

Vhitrigg Community Woodland

eam power. At its peak in 1952, it
nployed 1208 workers. It closed in 1972.
Bear left at the fork to enter conifer
oodland and right at the next fork,
ssing a fenced-off area containing
cular brick-built pools, before arriving at
gate. Beyond the gate, cross the road to
ad up a narrow avenue of conifer trees.
As the trees thin, bear right at the fork
d left at the next fork, following the
gn for the railway path to emerge from
e bushes at the top of the bing. Rather
surprisingly, there is a dog cemetery here. There are also excellent views across West Lothian towards the Five Sisters, West Calder and the Pentlands.

Take the path diagonally right to cross the top of the bing, bearing left to go across a crosspaths and downhill through heather and grassland. At the bottom of the hill, the track leads into the bushes to arrive at a junction. Turn right, picking up the railway path again to return to the start of the walk.

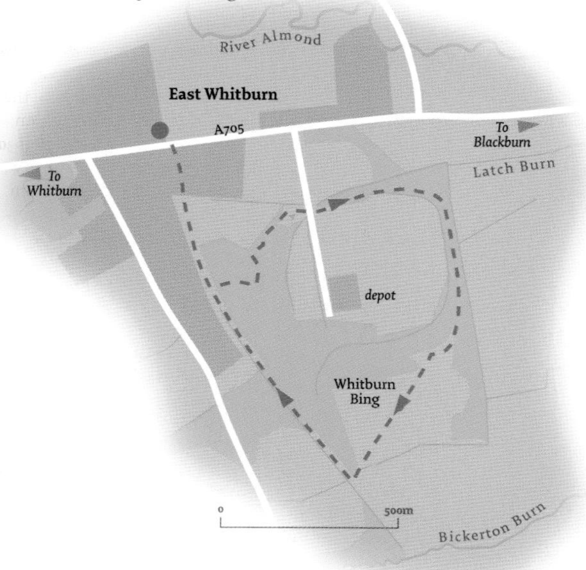

Fauldhouse Forest

Distance 3.5km Time 1 hour
Terrain good surfaced paths and unsurfaced tracks Map OS Explorer 343
Access regular bus and rail services to Fauldhouse from Livingston

Fauldhouse Moor was once home to several pits and quarries and was at the heart of the local coalmining industry. After the last of the collieries closed in 1957, the area was planted with coniferous trees and has since become home to a wide range of wildlife.

This walk follows the route of a former single-track mineral railway, the Fauldhouse (Benthead) Branch, which was part of the Wilsontown, Morningside and Coltness Railway. It ran from Fauldhouse onto Fauldhouse Moor, providing access to Benthead Mine, Benthead Quarry, Fallahill Colliery and Fauldhouse Colliery. The line was closed by 1922.

The route starts at the bottom of Harthill Road in Fauldhouse. Follow this road up the hill, crossing over Church Place and passing Falla Hill Primary School. Just beyond the school, turn rig onto a wide, straight path, going past some pigeon lofts and skirting around a green metal barrier. At the end of the path, turn left and follow a trail around the edge of a playing field. Turn left just before another green metal barrier.

Running parallel to another path a few metres over to the right, the track heads straight on. To the left, a field of young firs disappears into the distance. Turn le at the next T-junction. The track, wide a lined with brambles, swings very gently the left to arrive at a bench at a fork in th path. Bear right here to enter the forest. Rowan trees have taken root randomly alongside the trail, but the forest is mos tall closely planted conifers.

Fauldhouse Forest

The track winds its way through the
oodland where the shade of the trees
nd the damp ground encourages a
scinating and colourful explosion of
ıngi in the early autumn.

Soon the forest starts to thin. Reaching
junction at an information board, turn
the left to leave the line of the former
ailway and head back through the trees.
here is a less formal feel to this area as
he conifers are joined by brambles,
cots pine, raspberries and more
broadleaf trees with the forest floor a
carpet of heather.

Bear right at the next fork to exit
the forest and head past a small pond on
the right and deciduous trees such as
rowan, birch and hawthorn. The view
begins to open out here, revealing rolling
fields across the Breich Valley to the
distant Pentland Hills.

Reaching a junction at the end of
the path, turn right to go past the green
metal barrier and back to the start.

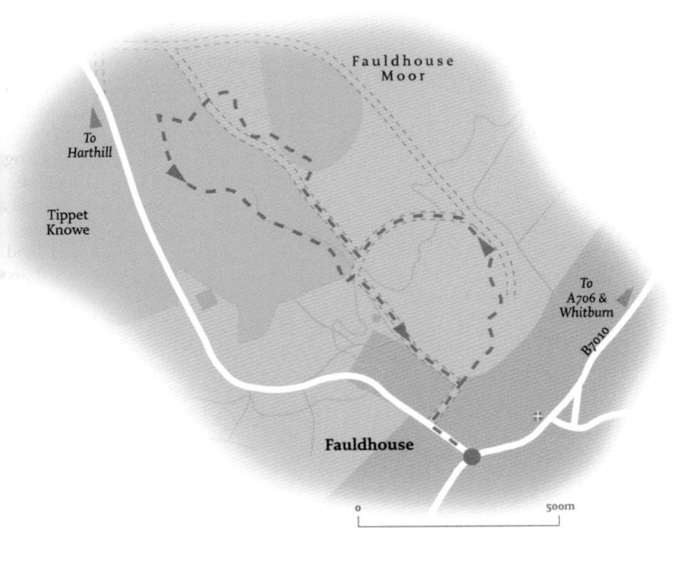

The Longridge loop

Distance **6.5km** Time **1 hour 45**
Terrain **good surfaced paths and unsurfaced tracks** Map **OS Explorer 343**
Access **regular bus and rail services to Fauldhouse from Livingston**

The Wilsontown, Morningside and Coltness Railway carried minerals such as ironstone, limestone and splint coal, hewn from beneath the bleak moorland of Central Scotland on a line that ran from Morningside (near Newmains), passing south of Shotts and terminating at Longridge, just east of Fauldhouse. This is an easy walk along the former railway line.

Starting just off the Main Street on the corner of Sheephousehill in Fauldhouse, walk up the hill and out of town. Continue along the path on the left side of the road to reach a set of traffic lights. Turn right to cross the road at the pedestrian crossing and follow the sign for Lanark. Continue until you reach the sign for the railway path to Fauldhouse.

The track from the road is the original entrance to Longridge Station and the remains of the platform can still be found nestling amongst the undergrowth. The railway began a passenger service soon after opening in 1845 and was absorbed by the Edinburgh and Glasgow Railway in 1849 before being extended to join the Bathgate to Edinburgh Line the following year to take advantage of the nascent shale oil industry. By 1930, the line was owned by the LNER, who withdrew passenger services. Their successor, British Railways, closed the route completely in 1963.

The line of the former railway runs
easantly through woodland of
wthorn, oak, sycamore and beech.
ıspberries line the edge of the track.
Continue straight ahead at a staggered
ossroads to pass underneath an old
idge, through a railway cutting and
neath another old bridge to enter the
ıtskirts of Fauldhouse. Go through a
teway and across a bridge, following
sign for Shotts Road.

Passing a grassy field, the track becomes
aggregate surfaced path. Reaching a
ad at the end of the path, turn right to
ive at a T-junction. Cross the road
aight ahead and go through a gateway
rejoin the railway path. At the fork, bear
t to cross a burn. Go through a gateway
d continue straight ahead.

Arriving at a road, turn right, then
nost immediately left to double back
and swing to the right to join the railway path again. This was the site of Crofthead Station. It opened in 1846 and was closed in 1930 when passenger services ceased.

The path passes Greenburn Golf Course on the left. The course has been in the present location since 1953 and was designed and built by the members of the club themselves.

At a crosspaths, go straight across. Reaching another gateway, follow the path to run parallel to the main Edinburgh to Glasgow Railway for a little way before bearing right to head down to the main road.

Pass around the side of a gateway and turn right to follow the main road back to the start.

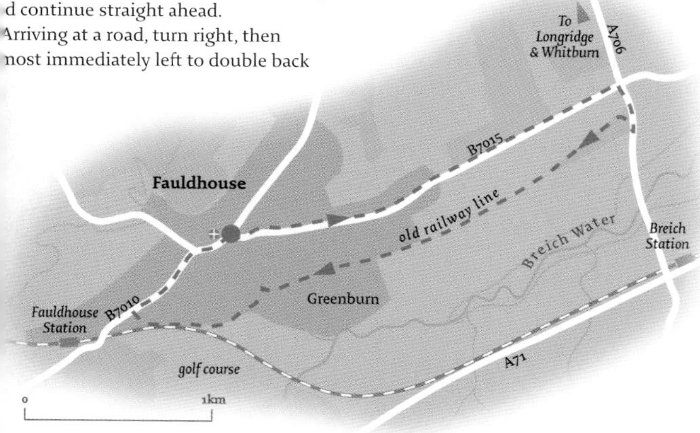

railway bridge over the former Wilsontown, Morningside and Coltness Railway

The Thieves Road and East Cairn

Distance 15km **Time** 3 hours 45
Terrain some surfaced roads, but mostly rough hill tracks, sometimes very boggy; very steep climb to the top of the hill
Map OS Explorer 344 **Access** no public transport to Harperrig or Little Vantage

Early cartographers did not usually include drove roads in their work, but this route through the Pentland Hills is shown in maps of the 18th and 19th centuries, illustrating its importance. It is known as the Thieves Road because of its popularity with the cattle-rustling Border Reivers who galloped over it on audacious night raids. Follow this ancient route to reach a Bronze Age cairn at West Lothian's highest point.

The walk starts at the fishing car park just down a minor road off the A70 between Carnwath and Balerno.

(An alternative start point is at the small car park at Little Vantage, following the Thieves Road from there and missing the castle and the reservoir entirely.)

From the car park, head towards Cairns Castle, crossing the Water of Leith and following the sign for Little Vantage through a gate and around the castle. George de Crychtoun is thought to have built the castle in around 1440 to guard the pass over the Pentlands, with the Water of Leith to the west and a burn to the south affording it some protection. The castle is now a ruin. The still extant main tower was attached to a secondary tower, which was removed in around 187 to be replaced by Cairns House, the adjacent private farmhouse.

Follow the Pentland Path waymarkers along the often boggy southern shore of the reservoir, crossing a stile to pass a

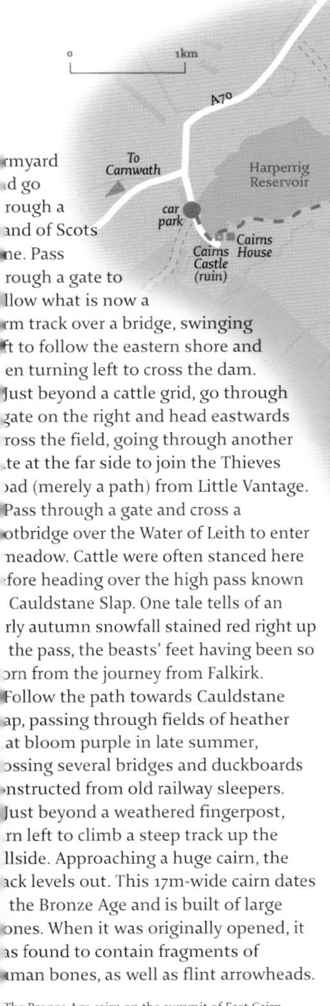

rmyard
ıd go
rough a
and of Scots
ne. Pass
rough a gate to
llow what is now a
rm track over a bridge, swinging
ft to follow the eastern shore and
en turning left to cross the dam.
Just beyond a cattle grid, go through
gate on the right and head eastwards
ross the field, going through another
te at the far side to join the Thieves
ɔad (merely a path) from Little Vantage.
Pass through a gate and cross a
otbridge over the Water of Leith to enter
neadow. Cattle were often stanced here
fore heading over the high pass known
Cauldstane Slap. One tale tells of an
rly autumn snowfall stained red right up
the pass, the beasts' feet having been so
ɔrn from the journey from Falkirk.
Follow the path towards Cauldstane
ap, passing through fields of heather
at bloom purple in late summer,
ɔssing several bridges and duckboards
nstructed from old railway sleepers.
Just beyond a weathered fingerpost,
rn left to climb a steep track up the
llside. Approaching a huge cairn, the
ack levels out. This 17m-wide cairn dates
the Bronze Age and is built of large
ones. When it was originally opened, it
as found to contain fragments of
ıman bones, as well as flint arrowheads.
It must have been the grave of someone of great importance.

Beyond the cairn, continue straight ahead past a smaller cairn and a fence corner, following an extremely boggy path up along the fence and through a gate, continuing for another 150m to the top of the hill, which is unmarked.

Retrace your steps to the small cairn and turn left, heading downhill and up a small slope to reach Cauldstane Slap. An illegal Covenanter sermon, or 'conventicle', was held here on 1 June 1684. General Tam Dalyell of the Binns and his troop were ordered to apprehend the men of the congregation, who were ready with blunderbusses, swords and pistols, but by the time they arrived, the Covenanters had disappeared into the hillside. Follow the path downhill to return to Harperrig.

The Bronze Age cairn on the summit of East Cairn

Craigengar

Distance 12km Time 3 hours
Terrain boggy moorland sheep tracks
Map OS Explorer 344 Access no public transport to Crosswood Reservoir

This strenuous walk across open moorland to reach the boundary of West Lothian is not for the faint of heart – it can get very boggy – but the views from the summit are worth it.

Crosswood Reservoir, where this route begins, is off the A70 midway between Balerno, on the outskirts of Edinburgh, and Carnwath in Lanarkshire. This elevated winding road over the moors is better known as the 'Lang Whang', a *whang* in Scots being a 'leather bootlace'.

Start on the access road to the reservoir, on the Public Right of Way to West Linton and Dolphinton. The reservoir was designed by the engineer James Leslie for the Edinburgh Water Company to complement Harperrig Reservoir and was completed in 1868. Leslie had studied the findings of an inquest into a dam that had burst in Yorkshire in 1852 and, as a result, this was one of the best-designed dams in the country.

Walk along the road to go through a gate following the Scotways waymarks past a line of telegraph poles. At the final pole, strike off to the right to cross two stiles and cross a field, aiming for a fingerpost. Turn left at the post, following the edge of the field to go through a gate and along the farm track by Mid Crosswood.

Go through another gate and follow a raised track uphill. Just beyond a junction leave the track to head east before swinging south to follow a grassy track up a narrow strip of land between fences. Cross the stile at the top and continue straight ahead across the boggy ground a a series of fingerposts to reach a stile over a drystane dyke. Listen out for curlews and grouse. Buzzards and kestrels also frequent the moors.

Instead of crossing the stile, head

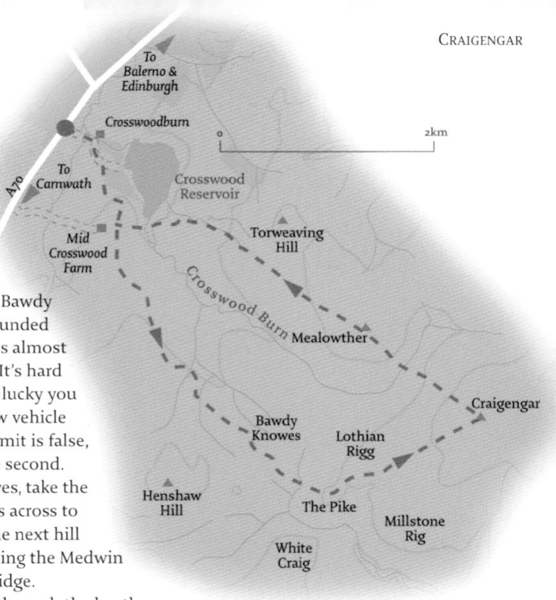

ooking north
rom Craigengar

wnhill to cross
hall Burn, then
urn to the dyke
d turn left to
low it across the
ssocks and bog of Bawdy
oss towards the rounded
l of Bawdy Knowes almost
mediately ahead. It's hard
ing, but if you are lucky you
ay be able to follow vehicle
cks. The first summit is false,
t soldier on to the second.
rom Bawdy Knowes, take the
eep track that runs across to
e Pike, which is the next hill
aight ahead, crossing the Medwin
ter by a rickety bridge.
t is a short climb through the heather
the top of The Pike, where there is a
all cairn of a dozen or so large stones.
ike out east to follow the fence across
heather-clad moorland of Lothian
gg towards the summit of Craigengar.
is fence marks the boundary between
st Lothian and the Scottish Borders.
hree fences meet at the summit of
aigengar, which has an austere beauty,
side the remains of an old wall and
me rocky outcrops. On a clear day, the
w is superb. To the northeast, the
ntlands stretch out towards Edinburgh.
the south, West Water Reservoir sits
side Catstone, with Black Law to the
uthwest. And to the north the Central
t sits in front of the hills of the Southern Highlands, stretching from Ben Lomond and the Arrochar Alps, Ben More and Stob Binnein in the Crianlarich Hills to Stuc a'Chroin and Ben Vorlich.

From the summit, follow the fence northwest in a straight line across thick heather to descend from Craigengar. At the bottom of the hill, cross the Crosswood Burn and leave the heather behind to follow the fence up the next hill, Mealowther, and down the other side.

Reaching a fence, turn left to follow it until it meets a track, and take this downhill. Cross the bridge over the burn and go through a gate to arrive back at Mid Crosswood, retracing your steps to the start at the reservoir.

The Covenanter's Grave

Distance 13.6 km **Time** 3 hours 30
Terrain boggy moorland sheep tracks
Map OS Explorer 344 **Access** no public transport to Crosswood Reservoir

A challenging trek across moorland to a remote Covenanter's grave. The usual way to this lonely spot is from the south, but this alternative begins at the northern end of the same traditional route across the Pentlands. It can be difficult walking at times and progress can be slow, but in good weather this landscape is quietly stunning.

Start from the access road to Crosswood Reservoir off the Lang Whang (A70), midway between Balerno and Carnwath.

Walk along the road to go through a gate, following the Scotways waymarks past a line of telegraph poles. At the final pole, strike off to the right to cross two stiles ar cross a field, aiming for a fingerpost. Turn left at the post, following the edge of the field to go through a gate and along the farm track by Mid Crosswood.

Go through another gate and follow a raised track uphill. Just beyond a junctio leave the track to head east before swinging south to follow a grassy track up a narrow strip of land between fences. Cross the stile at the top and continue straight ahead across the boggy ground a a series of fingerposts to reach a stile ove a drystane dyke.

After crossing this stile, turn left to cross the Small Burn. Follow more fingerposts towards Hainshaw Hill, a small hill on the horizon with a fallen tre

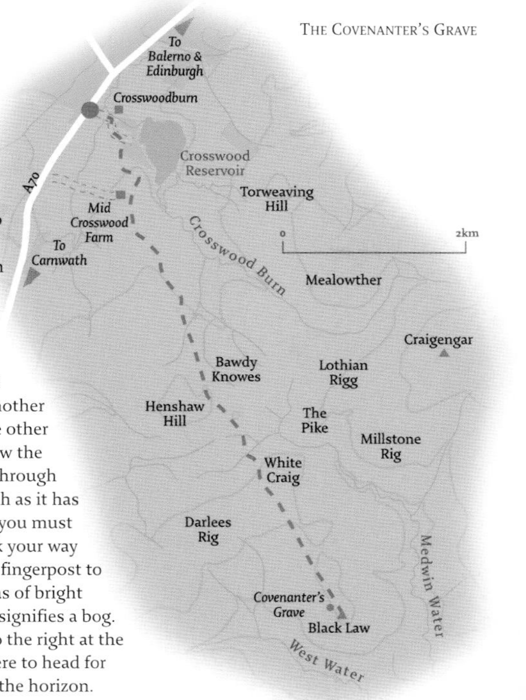

top, along with a low
ıare wall. Descend
ıtheast from the hilltop
go through a gate,
ssing from West Lothian
:o South Lanarkshire.
Aiming for the bealach
tween White Craig and
rlees Rig, the two hills
ectly to the south, head
wnhill to go through another
te and up the hill on the other
le, swinging left to follow the
ck a few metres uphill through
e heather. The track, such as it has
en, peters out here and you must
low sheep tracks to pick your way
rough the heather from fingerpost to
gerpost. Be wary of areas of bright
een moss – this usually signifies a bog.
The next fingerpost is to the right at the
o of the hill. Turn left here to head for
ıat looks like a cairn on the horizon.
ı closer inspection, it looks more like a
ıkeshift grave. Continue to follow the
gerposts up and over the bealach. The
venanter Donald Cargill is believed to
ve preached his final sermon at a
nventicle here on 10 July 1681. He was
ptured the next day, sentenced to death
d hanged soon after in Edinburgh.
There are five fingerposts after the
alach. Around 100m before the sixth,
ar the summit of Black Law, is the grave
John Carphin of Ayrshire, a Covenanter
ıo fought against General Tam Dalyell's
dragoons at the Battle of Rullion Green on 27 November 1666. That night, Adam Sanderson, a shepherd from Blackhill, near Medwynhead, answered his door to the badly wounded fugitive. Carphin refused to enter but allowed Sanderson to help him to the West Water as his dying wish was to be buried 'within sight of the Ayrshire hills'. A memorial stone was later placed where he fell. The present stone was erected in 1841. Retrace your steps from here to the start.

ohn Carphin's Grave

Index